Recipes from the
Gourmet Knitter

Robin Turner

Special Thanks

Dedicated to my family.
Thank you for inspiring me to realize all my dreams.

MODEL PHOTOGRAPHY: Maxwell Turner
DESIGN: Jolene Carey
ADDITIONAL PHOTOGRAPHY:
Wendy Fisher Art and Photography
MODELS: Ali Bernstein, Angelica Ciminella, Anna
Gusselnikova, Sophia Gutshall, Brittney Head, Cassie
Kenney, Jack McAllister, Clara Nuñez, Emma Richter,
Jude Schmalenberger, Alice Waters

Library of Congress Cataloging-in-Publication Data
Turner, Robin.
    Recipes from the gourmet knitter / Robin Turner
    p. cm.
    Includes bibliographical references and index.
    ISBN 978-0-615-54752-7
    1. Knitting – Patterns.
      I. Title: Recipes from the gourmet knitter.
      II. Title

10 9 8 7 6 5 4 3 2 1

Published by Great Balls of Yarn, Inc.
319 Belvedere Road,, West Palm Beach, FL 33405
United States of America

First Paperback Edition 2011
copyright 2011, Robin Turner

Distributed by Great Balls of Yarn, Inc.
Telephone: 561-651-1225
Fax: 561-651-1226
Email: info@greatballsofyarn.com
Web: www.greatballsofyarn.com

ISBN 978-0-615-54752-7

I've always loved the fiber arts and when my husband, Ray Holland, encouraged me to launch the opening of our flagship store in West Palm Beach, Florida, I had seriously underestimated how much time and effort goes into designing samples and building a team of knowledgeable and friendly instructors to aid and encourage our clientele. Our business has grown to multiple locations in South Florida only because of the fantastic and genuinely dedicated corps of talented women who work with me to run the daily operation of our stores. They are selfless, generous, good-natured souls who work incredibly hard to make our Great Balls of Yarn boutiques a special experience for those who visit us. I'm humbled by their dedication and am so appreciative to have our amazing team of "Yarnistas" inspire me every day with their knitting ability, acumen, designs, and creativity. You all are so special to me and I thank you!

To two people who really gave me my start, Stuart Berg and Betty Podlesh. When Ray and I first conceived the idea of building a business around knitting, the two of you were there from day one to share your insight and guidance with me. I am and will always be grateful for your encouragement and ideas.

To my son, Maxwell, your photography dazzles me. I've loved working on this project with you and am so proud of your talent, your work ethic and generally, what a dynamite human being you are.

Thank you to a special friend not only to me, but also to our entire industry: Barry Klein, owner of the innovative Trendsetter Yarns based in Los Angeles. Barry, you're never afraid to take a chance and I so appreciate everything you've done with us. We've shared a lot of laughs along the way. You always inspire me and I thank you for contributing two gorgeous designs to this book.

Also, special thanks to Nancy Boccuzzi, another friend and designer from NYC-based Lucci Yarns. You put the sparkle and glitz not only into yarns but the people you encounter each day. Thank you for also contributing your beautiful pattern to our book.

I'd also like to recognize and thank the following contributing designers and knitters from our team.

Marla Beck	Fran Herman	Susan Russell
Rebecca Cuevas	Elena Houmans	Susan Safian
Rochelle Casper	Raeann Kilman	Roberta Sirull
Harriet Elliot	Betty Podlesh	Anne Sloop
Evy Feiner	Olga Ramsey	Elizabeth Willard

Contents

Introduction

Two passions that capture my imagination are cooking a delicious meal and creating wearable art though knitting and crochet. A common denominator that these two past-times share is this: You must embark on each recipe with the finest ingredients.

Fortunately, I own a gourmet knitting store! Exquisite yarns and beautiful fibers, arranged by the color wheel, entice me seven days a week. Temptation waits each time I unlock the front door. Everyday is like walking through a candy store without the calories!

From the simplest strand of cashmere to a sparkly, sequined novelty concoction, each yarn almost calls out, begging to be touched. Just as a juicy red strawberry should be paired with a crème fraiche, certain patterns are more suitably paired with certain fibers. For instance, the gentle, flowing drape of a shawl pattern is achieved much easier with a hand-dyed rayon or a fine mohair as opposed to a stiff cotton. These are tricks of the trade that you learn through the experience of working in a knitting store.

In this book, we hope to inspire you with popular selections, proven recipes if you will, that our Great Balls of Yarn boutique clients have embraced and made into heirlooms to treasure for years to come. Many of the patterns we share in this book are created with our exclusive private label yarns from Robin Turner Gourmet Fibers. We've designed a few patterns that use "showcase yarns," those special fibers that we source from around the globe and hold dear. While we're always willing to kit each project for you, we've included the weight and composition of each yarn in the resource section of this book so that if you choose to substitute from your stash, or support your own local yarn store, you can still create a beautiful piece of wearable art.

We hope you're inspired by our designs and we encourage you to experiment and create your own treasured heirlooms. Gourmet cooking and the fiber arts can enrich your life for decades as they both combine art and science to yield a tangible, gratifying, and exciting result. Bon Appetit and Happy Knitting!

SWEET DREAMS

MATERIALS
3(3, 3, 4, 4) skeins each in two colors Robin Turner
Gourmet Fibers' Soft Dreams (model shown in (A) Light
Blue and (B) Lavender)
1 skein Robin Turner Back to Basics' Prima Pima to match

NEEDLES
Size 7
One 16 inch size 6 circular needle

GAUGE
20 sts and 28 rows = 4 inches in stockinette
stitch worked up on larger needles

FINISHED CHEST MEASUREMENT
Small   36 inches
Medium   40 inches
Large   44 inches
Extra Large   48 inches

NOTE
The front and back are worked together using the
intarsia method. Be certain to twist the colors together
when changing colors on the WS to avoid holes.

Continued on page 65

PAELLA DE VALENCIA

½ pint of Extra Virgin olive oil
12 mussels
12 clams
2 teaspoons minced garlic
1 large finely diced onion
1 medium tomato, skinned, seeded and chopped
1 small red pepper, seeded and cut into thin strips
1 small green bell pepper, seeded and cut into thin strips
1 small yellow bell pepper, seeded and cut into thin strips
32 oz skinless, boneless chicken breasts, cut into chunks
Salt and pepper to taste
1 teaspoon paprika
½ teaspoon dried rosemary
½ teaspoon dried thyme
¼ teaspoon ground cumin
12 uncooked squid ringlets/pieces
24 oz rice
3 cups chicken broth
¼ teaspoon saffron
2 chorizo sausages, cooked and cut into chunks
10 uncooked shrimp, peeled and de-veined
4 oz peas
4 tablespoons capers

Scrub the mussels and clams, discarding any that don't close when tapped sharply. Set aside. Heat 1/4 cup of the olive oil in a skillet. Add the pork, and brown all sides. Mix in the garlic, onions, tomato, and bell peppers, stirring constantly until cooked. Set aside. In another skillet, heat a further ¼ cup of olive oil and cook the chicken until browned on all sides. Season with salt, pepper, paprika, rosemary, thyme, and cumin. Transfer the chicken to a plate and set aside. Preheat the oven to 200 ºF. Heat 4 tablespoons olive oil in a skillet, and sauté the rice until it's translucent. Pour in the chicken broth and combine well. Add the pork mixture, stirring constantly. Sprinkle in the saffron and continue to stir until well mixed. Transfer the rice into a paella pan. Mix in the squid, chicken, chorizo sausages, mussels, clams, shrimp, peas, and capers, combining well. Bake the paella, uncovered, and on the lowest oven shelf, for approximately 25 minutes, or until all the liquid has been absorbed.

MAY DAY RUFFLED SUNTOP

MATERIALS
One skein each in three different colors Robin Turner Back to Basics' Prima Pima Model shown in Lime (A), Melon (B) and Sun (C)

NEEDLES
One 24 inch
   size 6 circular needle
One 24 inch
   size 7 circular needle

GAUGE
5 ½ sts = 1 inch on size 6 needle worked in stockinette

DESIGNER NOTES
Three ruffles are worked one at a time, then joined to the previous one worked. Back, Straps and Front are worked separately after ruffles are completed.

FINISHED CHEST MEASUREMENT
3 to 6 months   17 inches
6 to 12 months   18 inches
12 to 18 months   19 inches
18 to 24 months   20 inches

LENGTH TO UNDERARM
3 to 6 months   6 inches
6 to 12 months   7 ½ inches
12 to 18 months   9 inches
18 to 24 months   10 ½ inches

BOTTOM RUFFLE
Using color A and larger needle, CO 110 (116, 122, 128) sts. Join work in the round, being careful not to twist stitches. Begin garter st (Knit one round, Purl one round) and work even for 4 rounds. Change to stockinette (knit every round). Work even until piece measure 2 (2 ½ , 3, 3 ½) inches from the CO edge, while at the same time, decreasing 6 sts evenly spaced on the last round. 104 (110, 116, 122) sts remain. Change to smaller needle and continue in stockinette, work even until piece measures 4 (5, 6, 7) inches from CO edge, while at the same time, decrease 6 sts evenly on last round. 98 (104, 110, 116) sts remain. Set aside.

MIDDLE RUFFLE
Using color B and larger needle, CO 104 (110, 116, 122) sts. Work as for bottom ruffle until piece measures 2 (2 ½, 3, 3 ½) inches from CO edge, while at the same time, decrease 6 sts evenly spaced on last round. (98, 104, 110, 116) sts remain. Place this ruffle over the top of the first ruffle, aligning stitches with the stitches of the first ruffle. Join pieces by knitting 1 st from each piece together around. Change to smaller round needle and complete as for bottom ruffle (92, 98, 104, 110) stitches remain. Set aside.

TOP RUFFLE
Using color C and larger needle, CO 98 (104, 110, 116) stitches. Work as for middle ruffle until piece measure 2 (2 ½, 3, 3 ½) inches from CO edge, while at the same time, decrease 6 sts evenly spaced across the round. (92, 98, 104, 110) stitches remain. Place this ruffle over the top of the second ruffle and join as before.

Continued on page 65

10

SILKY MERINO DOUBLEKNIT CAPELET

MATERIALS
4 (5, 6) skeins Malabrigo Silky Merino (shown in Helechos)

NEEDLES
Size 11

DESIGNER NOTES
This pattern is a double-knitted stitch repeat. If you make an error in your work, try to refrain from ripping it back. It's very difficult to re-needle the work and you will be left guessing as to where to begin. Instead, unknit your work back to the error—even if it takes a few rows. You will be glad you did!

MAX'S WORLD-FAMOUS GUACAMOLE

4 ripe Mexican avocados
1 clove of garlic, minced
1/4 cup white onion, minced
1 jalapeño, minced
1 tomato, chopped
1 tablespoon salt
Juice from one lime

This pattern showcases the luminosity and vibrancy that only Malabrigo can create through the hand-painted artistry of their Silky Merino. Choose from an incredible palette of colorways and create a one-of-a-kind capelet that you'll enjoy for years.

FINISHED MEASUREMENTS
Small	10 by 50 inches
Medium	11 by 52 inches
Large	12 by 54 inches

ROW ONE
S1, *YO, K1, Repeat from* until end of row.
37 (41, 49) sts on needle.

ROW TWO
S1, *S1, YO, K1, Repeat from* until end of row.
55 (61, 73) sts on needle.

ROW THREE
S1, *S1, YO, K2TOG, Repeat from* until end of row.
55 (61, 73) sts on needle.

Repeat Row Three until desired length. You can measure the piece against your body if knitting on a circular needle.

Cast off over 2 rows.
Row One Cast Off: S1, *S1, K1, Repeat from* until end of row.
Row Two Cast Off: Bind off all stitches loosely.

FINISHING
Fold the short side of the piece so that it meets the bottom part of the longer opposite side. Loosely sew the edges together, creating a gently fold-over collar. Weave in ends.

Peel and pit avocadoes. Scoop out the pulp. Place in a medium-size bowl and mash the avocado with a fork so that the mixture is a bit chunky. Add the tomato, onion, garlic powder, and salt. Add in lime juice and mix all together. Serve with crisp tortilla chips.

GORGEOUS, LUSCIOUS MOCK CABLE SHRUG

SIZES

Small	34-38 inches
Medium	40-44 inches
Large	45-48 inches

Using size 9 circular needles and long-tail cast on, CO 168 (192, 216) sts.

Row 1: (WS) P2, *K4, P4 to last 6 sts, end K4, P2

Row 2: (RS) K2, *P4, K4 to last 6 sts, end P4, K2.

Repeat these 2 rows until piece measures 7 (8, 8) inches from CO edge. End by working a RS row.

Next row: Rib 30 as established, place marker, rib to last 30 sts, place marker, rib to end.

Dec row: Change to size 6 needles. (RS) K2 TOG, *(P2TOG) twice, (K2TOG) twice*. Rep between * once more, P2TOG twice, slip marker, **K1, K2TOG, K1, (P2TOG) twice** and repeat between ** to 4 sts before second marker, K1, K2TOG, K1, slip marker, (P2TOG) twice, (K2TOG) twice to last 6 sts, P2TOG twice, K2TOG.

SET NEW RIB PATTERN

Continue as follows:

Row 1 (WS): Rib as established across row.

Row 2 (RS): Rib to marker, *Sl1, K2, psso the 2 knitted sts, P2,. Repeat from * to 3 sts before marker, Sl1, K2, psso, slip marker, rib to end

Row 3 (WS): Rib to marker, slip marker,* P1, YO, P1, K2* repeat between * to 2 sts before marker, P1, YO, P1, slip marker, rib to end

Row 4 (RS): Rib as established

Row 5 (WS): Rib as established

Repeat rows 2 through 5 until pattern panel measures 17 (18, 19) inches.

End by working row 5.

MATERIALS

3 (4, 5) ASLANTRENDS Invernal (shown in Fuschia)

NEEDLES

One 24 inch size 6 circular needle
One 24 inch size 9 circular needle

GAUGE

4 sts=1 inch over rib pattern in larger needles
16 sts =4 inches in stockinette in smaller needles

DESIGNER NOTE

This is a close fitting garment. Above are bust size measurements for sizing guidance, not finished measurements.

Continued on page 66

GENTLEMAN'S CLASSIC ALPACA SCARF

Spoil the man you love with an amazingly soft and luxurious scarf this holiday season. Our Bolivian Alpaca will keep him toasty whether he's walking down the blustery streets of the city or taking in a spirited stadium football game. A timeless classic.

MATERIALS
3 skeins Robin Turner Gourmet Fibers' Bolivian Alpaca model shown in Light Grey

NEEDLES
Size 15

DESIGNER NOTES
Hold three strands of yarn together throughout pattern. When finished, fill a basin with slightly warm water and a good squirt of your favorite hair conditioner. Submerge scarf in basin and gently agitate. Roll scarf up in dry towel to absorb moisture then dry flat. The fine alpaca fibers will gently bloom, resulting in a luxurious effect.

FINISHED DIMENSIONS
10 by 65 inches

MOSSED-RIB STITCH
Row 1: K3, P3, K1, P3, K1, P3, K1, P3, K1, P3, K3
Row 2: K1, *P1, K1, repeat from * to end

With size 15 needles and holding 3 strands of yarn together, CO 25 sts loosely. Working garter stitch for 5 rows. Begin working in Mossed-Rib Stitch Pattern until scarf is 60 inches (or desired length). Work 5 rows in garter stitch. BO all stitches loosely. Weave in ends.

SUNDAY AFTERNOON FOOTBALL CHILI

3 pounds ground beef (or turkey)
1 1/2 cups chopped onion
3 cloves fresh garlic (crushed through press)
1 small green pepper, sliced and seeds removed
1 small red pepper, sliced and seeds removed
4 (15 ounce) cans kidney beans
4 (10.75 ounce) cans condensed tomato soup
8 cups tomato juice
3 teaspoons chili powder
Red Hot sauce to taste
1 packet Splenda
8 cups water
Sour cream
Green onions
salt to taste

In a large pot over medium heat, combine the ground beef (or turkey) onions, garlic and sliced peppers. Saute until meat is browned and vegetables are softened. Drain excess fat, beans, tomato soup, tomato juice, chili powder, water and salt to taste. Toss in Splenda, and Red Hot to your liking. Bring just to a boil and reduce heat to low. Simmer for 1 hour and serve. Garnish with a sour cream and sliced green onions.

PENN STATE STADIUM SCARF

You say Jo Pa! I say TERNO! Let's cheer on my alma mater, the Penn State Nittany Lions with this fabulous herringbone scarf! Using just one skein of Malabrigo's Rasta and size 19 needles, this easy and unusual woven-look knitted up in two hours flat! Score!!

FINISHED MEASUREMENTS
6 by 60 inches

DIRECTIONS
With Size 19 needle, cast on 10 sts loosely.
Row 1: K1, *S1, K1, PSSO but before dropping slipped stitch from LH needle, Knit into the back of it. Repeat from * to end, K1.
Row 2: *P2TOG, do not slip sts off needle. Purl first st again, Slip both sts off needle. Repeat from * to end.
Continue this two row pattern until desired length. BO loosely. Use remaining yarn for a rich fringe. Gently steam to block.

NOTE
Stitch is multiple of 2 so if a wider scarf is desired add stitches in increments of 2. Makes an interesting sweater pattern repeat too!

MATERIALS
One skein Malabrigo Rasta
Model Shown in Indiecita

NEEDLES
Size 19

LAS BRISAS GAZPACHO

¾ cup water
1 ½ pounds ripe tomatoes, chopped
¾ pound fresh tomatillos (called tomate verde in Mexico) husked and chopped
½ cup finely chopped white onion
1-2 fresh serrano chiles, chopped
  (remove seeds for less heat)
1 medium clove garlic, minced
1 tablespoon red wine vinegar
2 tablespoons Extra Virgin olive oil
Salt to taste
Chopped cucumber for garnish
Chopped red pepper for ganish
Chopped cilantro for garnish
Chopped avocado for garnish
Garlic croutons

Place water, 1 pound of the tomatoes, ½ pound of the tomatillos, half the onion, the chiles and the garlic in a blender. Puree until smooth.

Pour the pureed mixture into a large bowl and stir in the remaining chopped tomatoes and tomatillos, the vinegar, oil, and salt to taste. Add more vinegar to taste if desired. Thin with more water if desired. Chill for at least 30 minutes. Ladle into bowls. Garnish as desired. Yields 6 servings.

FUN AND FRILLY GIRL'S PONCHO

MATERIALS

1 (2,2,2) skeins Robin Turner Back to Basics' Prima Pima (model shown in Rose)
3 (3,4,4) balls Robin Turner Gourmet Fibers' Delizioso (model shown in Baby Pink)
One skein Trendsetter Cha Cha for ruffled trim. (model shown in Rose)

NEEDLES

Size 9

GAUGE

4 sts = one inch in pattern stitch with size 9 needles

DESIGNER NOTE

Hold one strand of Prima Pima and one strand of Delizioso throughout body of poncho

A marvelous project for a beginner knitter with the fun of something new!! Simply make two rectangles and join them together. The self-ruffling Cha Cha trim around the edge makes this a festive and unique poncho!

SIZING

Child Small	12 months to 3 years
Child Medium	4 to 6 years
Child Large	7 to 9 years
Child Extra Large	10 to 14 years

PATTERN STITCH

Row 1 (WS): K1, P1 across row
Row 2 (RS): K all sts across row

DIRECTIONS (Make two identical pieces)

With size 9 needle and holding two strands together as stated above, CO 40 (48, 52, 56) sts. Work in pattern stitch until each piece measures 18 (20, 22, 23) inches from CO edge.
Bind off loosely.

FINISHING

Place first piece vertically on table. Place second piece at bottom, horizontally. (This forms an L shape.) Join edges. Fold pieces toward you until the side edge of the horizontal piece (A) meets the top of the vertical piece (A). Join edges and weave in ends.

CHA CHA TRIM

With RS facing use one strand of Delizioso and pick up evenly along the perimeter of the poncho. Next Row: Begin carrying Cha Cha along with the Delizioso, knitting into the top squares ONLY of the Cha Cha, The Delizioso will stabilize the ruffle. Work 3 more rows then BO in the fourth row loosely.

OPTIONAL CHA CHA FLOWER

A cute embellishmet is to add a flower on the front. The flower is knitted the same way, in the top square of the Cha Cha. CO 8 sts with Delizioso, Next Row, knit with Cha Cha and Delizioso. Knit 3 more rows, then BO. Sew edges together to form rose and attach to poncho.

Innocent

REGAL RIBBON PONCHO

Pagewood Farm does it again! This unique hand-dyed ribbon and embellished Paparazzi worked up quickly to make a spirited design that we know will capture the imagination people everywhere.

SIZES One Size

KNITTED MEASUREMENTS
Width around lower edge - 54"
length from neck to bottom - 21"

PATTERN STITCH - CONDO STITCH
*Row 1 & 3: (RS) Knit, using Yarn A
Row 2 & 4: (WS) Purl using Yarn A
Row 5: (RS) with # 19 needle using Yarn B, Purl each stitch wrapping yarn around needle twice.
Row 6: (WS) with #11 needle using Yarn B, Knit each stitch dropping extra wraps*
Repeat this pattern from * to * carrying unused yarn up the side selvedge.

BACK
CO 28 stitches with #11 needle and Yarn A.
SET UP ROW: (WS) Purl 13 Stitches, PM, Purl 2, PM, Purl 13.
Begin PATTERN STITCH and at the same time M1 before 1st and after 2nd marker on each RS row (including wrapping rows). This will create a triangular shape.
Repeat pattern a total of 8 times (76 stitches)
(This is the point at which you can lengthen poncho by doing additional repeats of PATTERN STITCH.
Knit one row.
Purl one row.
Bind off very loosely.

FRONT Same as Back

FINISHING
Gently block to measurements. Using crochet hook and ribbon attach back to front at side seams.

MATERIALS
5 Skeins Pagewood Farms Hand Dyed Silk Ribbon in Periwinkle (Yarn A)
4 Skeins Pagewood Farms Paparazzi in Periwinkle (Yarn B)
24 or 32" #11 circular needle (or size that will give you proper gauge)

NEEDLES
One 32 inch
  size 11 circular needle
One pair
  size 19 straight needles

GAUGE
10 sts = 4" in stockinette stitch using size 11 needles or any size to get this gauge

NOTE
Piece is worked from top down. To add length simply do additional repeats of Condo Pattern until desired length. To increase width use larger needle for rows 1-4 of pattern stitch - yarn amounts will vary.

JUDE'S ENTRELAC BLANKET

FINISHED SIZE
28 by 35 inches

With size 8 needles, CO 84 sts.

Row 1 (RS):   Knit

Row 2 (WS): *P2, turn; K2,turn; P3, turn; P3, turn; K3, turn; P4, turn; K4, turn; P5, turn; K5, turn; P6, turn; K6,turn; P7 turn; K7, turn; P8, turn; K8, turn; P9, turn; K9, turn; P10, turn; K10, turn; P11, turn; K11, turn; P12. Repeat from* to end.

Row 3 (RS):   K2, turn; P2, turn; inc. in 1st st., S1, K1, psso, turn; P3, turn; inc. in 1st st., K1, S1, K1, psso, turn; P4, turn; inc. in 1st st., K2, Sl, K1, psso, turn; P5,turn; inc in 1st st, K3, Sl, K1, psso, turn; P6, turn; inc in 1st., st, K4, S1, K1,psso, turn; P7, turn; inc., in 1st st, K5, S1 K1, psso, turn; P8,turn; inc. in 1st st, K6, S1 K1, psso, turn; P9, turn; inc in 1st st, K7, S1, K1, psso, turn; P10,turn; inc in 1st st, K8, S1, K1, psso, turn; P11, turn; inc in 1st st, K9, S1, K1, psso,* pick up and knit 12 sts evenly down left side of diamond, working across these 12 sts and next 12 sts on left hand needle proceed as follows:
Turn; P12, turn; K11, S1, K1, psso. 12 times, rep from * to last diamond, pick up and knit 12 sts evenly down left side of last diamond, turn; P2tog, P10, turn; K11, turn; P2TOG, P9, turn; K10, turn, P2TOG, P8, turn; K9 turn, P2TOG, P7, turn; K8, turn; P2TOG, P6; turn, K7, turn; P2TOG, P5, turn; K6, turn; P2TOG, P4, turn; K5, turn; P2TOG, P3, turn; K4, turn; P2TOG, P2, turn; K3, turn; P2TOG, P1, turn; K2, turn; P2TOG.

Row 4 (WS): Pickup and purl 11 sts evenly down left side of diamond working across these 12 sts and next 12 sts on left hand needle proceed as follows:
Turn; K12, turn; P11, P2TOG, 12 times, *pick up and purl 12 sts evenly down left side of diamond, (turn; K12, turn; P11, P2TOG) 12 times rep from * to end.

MATERIALS
10 skeins Malabrigo Rios (model shown in Solis)

NEEDLES
One 24 inch
    size 7 circular needle
One 24 inch
    size 8 circular needle

Peace

Continued on page 66

ALPACA CABLE SWEATER

MATERIALS
4(5,5,6,7,8) skeins of Robin Turner Gourmet Fibers' Bolivian Alpaca

NEEDLES
One 36 inch
  size 9 circular needle
Cable needle

GAUGE
20 sts = 4" in cable pattern on size 9 needle

DESIGN NOTE
Sweater is worked side to side, beginning with right sleeve.

SIZES AND MEASUREMENTS

Extra Small	Chest 34 inches
Small	Chest 38 inches
Medium	Chest 42 inches
Large	Chest 46 inches
Extra Large	Chest 50 inches
Plus	Chest 54 inches

Length: 23(23, 23, 25 ¾, 27 ½, 271/2) inches
Upper Arm 19 ¼,(19 ¼, 19 ¼, 22½, 24, 24) inches

CABLE PATTERN STITCH
Definition of C8F – Sl 4 sts to cn, hold in front, K4, K4 from cn
Row 1 (RS): *C8F, K4; rep from * across
Row 2 and all WS Rows: Purl
Rows 3, 5, 7 & 9 : Knit
Row 10: Rep Row 2

RIB PATTERN STITCH
Row 1: *K3, P3; rep from * across
Row 2: Knit the knits, and purl the purl sts as the face you

RIGHT SLEEVE
With size 9 needles, CO 72(72,72,84,90,90)sts. Next Row (RS): Beg 3 x 3 rib pattern. Work even until piece measures 3 inches from CO edge, end after RS row.
Next Row (WS): Continue in pattern, inc 24(24,24,28,30,30) sts evenly across row as follows: work 2 sts in rib, inc 1 (kf&b or pf&b in pattern) rep from * across 96(96,96,112,120,120)sts.
Next Row (RS): Change to Stockinette; work 2 rows even, end after WS row.

ESTABLISH CABLE PATTERN
Next Row (RS): K2(2,2,4,2,2,), place marker (pm), work Row 1 of Cable pattern across to last 10(10,10,12,10,10)sts. C8F, pm, K2(2,2,4,2,2). Keeping sts between markers in Cable pattern, remaining sts in Stockinette. Work even till sleeve measures 4(4,4,5,5 ½,5 ½) inches from CO edge, end after WS row.

Continued on page 67

SILKY LLAMA COUNTRY CLUB STOLE

You'll fall in love all over again with our Silky Llama, a delicious blend of King Baby Llama and Mulberry Silk from Robin Turner Gourmet Fibers. Simply Divine! Choose to make the stole in a variety of hues like we did, or use all one color. Either way, you'll love knitting it as much as the end result.

FINISHED SIZE
22 by 60 inches before fringe

DIRECTIONS
With size 8 needles, CO 7 sts.
Row 1 (RS):   *K6, P2*, repeat from *to* until
              last 6 sts remain, K6
Row 2 (WS):   *P6, K2*, repeat from *to* until
              last 6 stitches remain, P6
Repeat Rows 1 and 2 until 60 inches or desired length. (If making multi-color version, change colors after 20 inches each.)

DROP STITCH AND BIND OFF
On last row work as follows: With RS facing, bind off the 6 knitted sts in pattern. Drop the next 2 stitches from the needle; turn work and CO 2 sts, binding them off as you create them. This will lock in the drop stitches and keep the work from puckering on the bind off edge. Turn work back to RS and continue the bind off using the same method until the end of the row. Gently encourage the stitches to drop all the way down the stole. Gently block with steam. Cut Hanah silk into 6 inch pieces and tie them on liberally along both edges. Lovely!

MATERIALS
3 skeins Robin Turner Gourmet Fibers' Silky Llama (shown in Crimson, Sugarplum and Moroccan Spice)
One half spool 1 ½" Hannah Hand Dyed Satin Ribbon to match

NEEDLES
Size 8

GAUGE:
4 sts = 1 inch in stockinette
  with size 8 needles

WAVE STITCH PULLOVER

Instructions are given for smallest size, with larger sizes in parentheses. When only one number is given, it applies to all sizes.

FINISHED MEASUREMENTS
Chest: 34-36 (38, 40)"
Length: 21 1/4 (22 1/2, 23 3/4)"

Row 1-4: SS, Garter Stitch (knit every row), SS.
Row 5: SS, *K4, YO, K1, YO, K1, YO twice, K1, YO twice, K1, YO 3 times, K1, YO 3 times, K1, YO 3 times, K1, YO 4 times, K1, YO 4 times, K1, YO 3 times, K1, YO 3 times, K1, YO 3 times, K1, YO twice, K1, YO twice, K1, YO, K1, YO, K1, K4*; repeat from *, end SS.
Row 6: SS, knit, dropping all YO's off needle, SS.
Row 7-10: SS, Garter Stitch (knit every row), SS.
Row 11: SS, * YO 4 times, K1, YO 3 times, K1, YO 3 times, K1, YO 3 times, K1, YO twice, K1, YO twice, K1, YO, K1, YO, K1, K8, YO, K1, YO, K1, YO twice, K1, YO twice, K1, YO 3 times, K1, YO 3 times, K1, YO 3 times, K1, YO 4 times, K1*; repeat from *, end SS.
Row 12: SS, knit, dropping all YO's off needle, SS.
Repeat rows 1-12.

MATERIALS
KoiguTM Painter's Palette Premium Merino Wool Yarn (KPPPM) (100% Merino Wool, 175 yards / 50 grams) in Deep Coral Pink: 6 (7, 8) skeins

NEEDLES
Size 4 (3.5mm) or size needed to obtain correct gauge
Tapestry needle or crochet cook (for finishing)

GAUGE
19 sts and 23 rows = 4" in Wave Stitch Pattern on needles US#4

Alternate Chart Written Instruction

NOTE
This method of working selvage (edge) stitches makes a chain stitch edge, with each chain loop representing two rows. Each row starts and ends with a selvage stitch. Right Side Rows: Slip the first stitch knitwise, work to the last stitch, and knit it. Wrong Side Rows: Slip the first stitch purlwise, work to the last stitch, and purl it. Repeat these two rows.

CHART

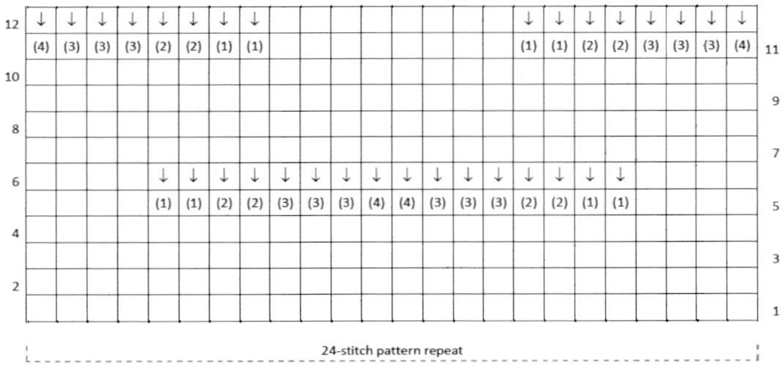

Chart is worked right to left on right side (odd) rows, and left to right on wrong side (even) rows.
Repeat rows 1-12

Symbols:

☐ K1 on both Right Side and Wrong Side	(3)	YO 3 times, K1
(1) YO, K1	(4)	YO 4 times, K1
(2) YO twice, K1	↓	knit, dropping all YO's off needle

Continued on page 67

31

PRINCESS ANNE

MATERIALS
2 (3) skeins Lucci Luca Tape
(model shown in White White
Gold)
2 stitch markers

NEEDLES
One 36 inch
  size 15 circular needle

DIFFICULTY
Advanced Beginner

POOLSIDE LOBSTER CITRUS SALAD

2 avocados halved, sliced into chunks
2 small lobster tails cooked
  and sliced into bite size chunks
Small bunch cilantro
  coarsely chopped
1 small grapefruit, sectioned
Chopped, cooked bacon slices
1 red onion, thinly sliced
  and broken apart
Mixed mesclun greens
Pine nuts
Extra Virgin Olive Oil
Balsamic Vinegar

SIZE
Small/Medium	43 inches wide by 18 1/2 inches long
Large/Extra Large	57 inches wide by 25 inches long

PATTERN STITCH
Rows 1,3,5,7,9 (RS):
K4, yo, K1, kf&b, K to marker, yo, slm (slip marker), K1, slm, yo, knit to last 6 sts, kf&b, K1, yo, K4. (6 sts increased each row)

Rows 2,4,6,8,10,12 (WS):
K4, purl to the last 4 sts, k4.

Row 11:
K4, (yo,K1)2x, *yo, K2TOG, repeat from * to m, yo, slm, K1, slm, yo, K1, repeat from * to last 5 sts, yo, K1,yo, K4.

DIRECTIONS
Cast on 15 sts.
Set up row: K4, P3, pm, P1, pm, P3, K4.
Begin pattern st and work for 3(4) repeats. 120 (155)

RUFFLE EDGE
Row 1: K1, kf&b in each stitch to one st before end, K1
Row 2: Purl
Row 3: Repeat Row 1
BO purlwise

Cover the avocado slices with juice from one grapefruit section to keep it from turning brown. Combine greens, cilantro and onion then place in chilled serving bowls. Add lobster, avocado and grapefruit slices on top. Garnish with bacon bites, pine nuts and remaining cilantro. Serve immediately with extra virgin olive oil and balsamic vinegar on the side.

STUNNING SEQUINED STOLE

Using one skein of Robin Turner Potpourri with Paillettes and a corresponding skein of Prism's Cool Stuff, we created this diagonal showstopper of a stole. Looks great with silk slacks for evening or pair it with casual khakis for a fun accessory!

Finished length from point to point 60 inches.

Cast on 55 sts loosely. Knit one row.
Begin pattern repeat to create diagonal.

DIAGONAL PATTERN REPEAT

ROW 1: Knit 1, Make 1, Work across row until last 2 sts remain, then K2TOG.
ROW 2: Work across row.

We used a combination of stitches while working in the pattern repeat. Because the yarns used for this design change as you knit them, we suggest straight garter stitch when bumpy, lashy, or textured yarns emerge from the skein. To add interest, we simply faggotted (YO, K2TOG across entire row, all while working diagonal pattern) when smooth, plain yarns emerged from skein.

Complete the stole by knitting the last 6 rows in straight garter (while still using Diagonal Pattern Repeat). Bind off last row loosely.

Slice artichoke tops off, crosswise. Trim stems. Steam artichokes until bottoms pierce easily, or a petal pulls off easily. Drain and cool. Cut each artichoke in half lengthwise and scrape out center and any purple tipped petals. Mix remaining ingredients in a large plastic bag. Place artichokes in the bag and coat all sides of the artichokes. Marinade at least one hour. Drain artichokes. Place cut side down on a grill over a solid bed of medium coals or gas grill on medium. Grill until lightly browned on the cut side, 5 to 7 minutes. Turn artichokes over and drizzle some of the remaining marinade over the artichokes. Grill until petal tips are lightly charred, 3 to 4 minutes more.

MATERIALS
1 skein Robin Turner Potpourri with Paillettes
1 skein Prism Cool Stuff
(or choose to use 2 skeins of the Potpourri with Paillettes)

NEEDLES
Size 10.5

DESIGNER'S NOTE
about the paillettes . . . simply guide the paillettes into place then knit the yarn. The paillettes will drop to the knit side. We used a five stitch pattern: Knit 5, place paillette, K5 across row. You can see how the paillettes gently fall into a diagonal line on the photo to the left.

GRILLED ARTICHOKES

4 large artichokes
¼ cup balsamic vinegar
¼ cup water
¼ cup low sodium soy sauce
¼ cup Extra Virgin olive oil
1 tablespoon minced ginger

DELIZIOSA TEE
with Picot cast-on edge

SIZES AND FINISHED MEASUREMENTS

Small   Bust 32 inches
Medium   Bus 36 inches
Large   Bust 40 inches
Extra Large   Bust 44 inches
Plus   Bust 48 inches
Extra Plus   Bust 52 inches

Length 22 ½ (22 ½-23-23 ½-24-24) inches

BACK

** Optional cast-on on Page 68**
With straight needles, cast on 82(92,102,112,122,132) sts. Work even in stockinette for 1 inch, end on RS. Knit the next row on WS for Garter Ridge. Work even in stockinette until piece measures 3 inches from beg, end on WS.

Dec Row (RS): K2, K2TOG, K to last 4 sts, SSK, K2 – 80(90,100,110,120,130) sts. Rep this dec every 2 inches twice more – 76(86,96,106,116,126) sts. Work even until piece measures 9 inches from beg, end on WS.

Inc Row (RS): K2, M1k, K to last 2 sts, M1k, K2 – 78(88,98,108,118,128) sts. Rep this inc every 2 inches twice more – 82(92,102,112,122,132) sts. Work even until piece measures 14 inches from beg, end on WS.

SHAPE ARMHOLES

Bind off 5(5,7,9,10,11) sts at beg of the next 2 rows – 72(82,88,94,102,110) sts.

Dec Row (RS): K2, K2TOG, K to last 4 sts, SSK, K2 – 70(80,86,92,100,108) sts. Rep this dec every RS row 5(8,8,9,10,12) times more – 60(64,70,74,80,84) sts. Work even until armholes measure 7 ½(7 ½,8,8 ½,9,9) inches, end on WS.

Continued on page 68

MATERIALS
4(5,6,6,7,7) balls of Robin Turner
Gourmet Fibers' Deliziosa

NEEDLES
Size 4

GAUGE
20 sts and 26 rows = 4" in
Stockinette on size 4 needles
TAKE TIME TO CHECK
GAUGE

ELIZABETH'S EASY CHILD'S VEST

SIZES

Small (Child 3 to 4)   Chest 24 inches
Medium (Child 5 to 6)   Chest 25 inches
Large (Child 7 to 8)   Chest 26 inches
Extra Large (Child 9 to 10) Chest 27 inches

DIRECTIONS

With size 8 needles and MC, cast on 42(44,48,52) sts.
Knit in stockinette for 24 rows. End with RS Row.
Change to circular needles. Knit RS row
Cast on 24 more sts, then pick-up 42(44,48,52) sts along
the cast-on edge, cast on 24 sts, Place marker.
Join work then begin working in the round.
Knit one round.

Next round. Kf&b in every stitch.
(doubling total stitch count.)

Change to CC and knit 2 rounds in 1x1 rib
Change to MC and knit 7 rounds in 1x1 rib
Change to CC and knit 2 rounds in 1x1 rib
Change to MC and knit 7 rounds in 1x1 rib
Change to CC and knit 2 rounds in 1x1 rib
Change to MC and knit 2 rounds in 1x1 rib.
Bind off in Rib pattern.

DIAGRAM

Picked up and
ribbed Stitches ....

BACK

MATERIALS

Robin Turner Back to Basics'
Microwash 3(3,4,4) MC, 1(1,1,2)
CC (model shown in Leafy Green
and White)

NEEDLES

Size 8 Straight
One 36 inch size 8 circular needle
Stitch Markers

GAUGE

14 sts = 4 inches in stockinette
stitch on size 8 needles

RAY'S FAVORITE CHOCOLATE PEANUT BUTTER CHIP COOKIES

2 cups all-purpose flour (sifted)
3/4 cup Hershey's Cocoa
1 teaspoon baking soda
1/2 teaspoon salt
1-1/4 cups (2-1/2 sticks)
    unsalted butter, softened
2 cups sugar
2 eggs
2 teaspoons vanilla extract
1-2/3 cups (10-oz. pkg.)
    Reese's Peanut Butter Chips

Heat oven to 350°F. Stir together flour, cocoa, baking soda and salt;
set aside. Beat butter and sugar in large bowl with mixer until fluffy.
Add eggs and vanilla; beat well. Gradually add flour mixture, beating
well. Stir in peanut butter chips. Drop by rounded teaspoons onto
ungreased cookie sheet. Bake 8 to 9 minutes. (Do not overbake;
cookies will be soft. They will puff while baking and flatten while
cooling.) Cool slightly; remove from cookie sheet to wire rack. Cool
completely. About 4 dozen cookies. Serve with ice cold skim milk and
watch them disappear!

PALM BEACH FANTABULOUS

MATERIALS
3 skeins Prism Kid Slique
(model shown in Freesia)
1 skein Prism Galaxy
(model shown in Freesia)

NEEDLES
Size 10 and 11

This could be the easiest and most elegant shawl ever! Done in a straight garter stitch with a lustrous hand-dye from Prism, this project comes alive when you deliberately drop every fifth stitch then weave Galaxy ribbon through the ladders. From strolling Worth Avenue to dining at Taboo, we guarantee you'll literally turn heads in this timeless classic!

With larger needles, loosely cast on 39 stitches. Switch to smaller needles and knit each row until almost all of last skein of Kid Slique is used. Switch back to larger needles then BO loosley as follows. BO 4 sts, drop one, BO 4 sts, drop one, BO 4 sts, drop one, BO 4 sts, drop one, BO 4 sts, drop one, BO 4 sts, drop one, BO 4 sts, drop one, BO last 4 sts. Secure and weave in ends.

FINISHING
With your fingers, run the dropped stitches all the way from the BO edge to the CO edge. There will be 7 rows. Gently weave the Galaxy ribbon it through the "back" of the ladder stitches in each of the 7 dropped stitch rows, leaving a long tail on each end. Make sure that the ribbon is not too tight, as you want it to lay flat. Secure ends and fringe liberally with remaining ribbon.

PALM BEACH MAHI MAHI TACOS

1 1/2 lb mahi mahi fillets cut
lengthwise into strips
1 cup flour
1 teaspoon salt
1/4 teaspoon ground black pepper
1 tablespoon vegetable oil
2 eggs, separated
Extra Virgin olive oil
    necessary for frying
Large corn tortillas, warmed

Raw onion sliced thin, marinated
in vinegar with a pinch of oregano
Max's World-Famous Guacamole
Fresh salsa
Fresh chopped cilantro

Pat the fish filet strips dry with paper towels. Mix the flour, salt, pepper, vegetable oil and egg yolks to form a batter. Beat the egg whites until stiff, and fold into the mixture. In a large skillet, heat oil to a depth of 1 inch. Dip each fish strip in the batter, fry quickly on one side, turning to fry the other until golden brown. (This only takes a couple of minutes on each side.) Drain on paper towels. Arrange pieces of fish in softened tortillas and serve at once, accompanied by fresh cilantro, marinated onions, guacamole, and salsa. Yields 6 servings.

HEAVENLY ANGORA BABY CABLE SCARF

MATERIALS
4 balls Robin Turner
Gourmet Fibers'
HEAVENLY ANGORA
model shown in Powder Blue

NEEDLES
size 10 ½

NOTE
Yarn is worked DOUBLE
STRANDED throughout
project. Also, slip the first
stitch of each row to create a
soft smooth edge.

Luscious! Luscious! Luscious! This affordable yet extravagant indulgence is equally wonderful to knit up as to wear! Worked in Robin Turner Gourmet Fibers' HEAVENLY ANGORA, this easy to create scarf looks soft and alluring on both sides.

FOUR ROW BABY CABLE PATTERN
Row 1: S1, K1, P2, *K2, P2, repeat from * to end of row.
Row 2: S1, P1, K2, *P2, K2, repeat from * to end of row.
Row 3: S1, K1, P2, *K2TOG but do not drop sts from left
          needle, k into first of these sts again, drop both sts from
          left needle, P2, repeat from * to end of row.
Row 4: Repeat row 2.

DIRECTIONS
CO 30 sts loosley. Establish Rib Pattern by working rows 1 and 2 twice, then work rows 3 and 4. Continue working Rows 1 to 4 repeatedly until scarf measures 50 inches. Finish by working Rows 1 and 2 twice to balance rib pattern at end. BO loosley. Weave in ends.

IRRESISTIBLE COCONUT MACAROONS

Butter and flour for preparing baking sheet and foil
1 large egg white
1 tablespoon sugar
1/4 teaspoon vanilla
1/8 teaspoon almond extract
3/4 cup sweetened flaked coconut

Put oven rack in middle position and preheat oven to 300°F. Butter a baking sheet, then line with foil and lightly butter and flour foil, knocking off excess flour. Stir together egg white, sugar, vanilla, almond extract, and a pinch of salt until combined, then fold in coconut. Divide coconut mixture into fourths, then drop in 4 mounds (about 2 inches apart) onto baking sheet. Bake until tops are pale golden in spots, 15 to 20 minutes, then carefully lift foil with cookies from baking sheet and transfer to a rack to cool.

Comfort

WHIMISCAL WEDDING HONEYMOON AFGHAN

Snuggle with your Sweetie or give this heirloom as a gift. This romantic decorator throw was created with all Prism Yarns and fringed with luxurious hand-dyed Hanah Satin which sets the colors off beautifully.

PATTERN SEQUENCE

(four row repeat)

Row 1: Knit
Row 2: Purl
Row 3: * K2TOG 3 times, (YO, K1) 6 times,
        K2TOG 3 times, repeat from *
Row 4: Knit

With Size 11 needle, loosely CO 180 stitches. Begin Pattern Sequence, changing yarns randomly throughout design. When afghan measures 40 inches, end on wrong side row and BO loosely. Finished size: 40 by 60 inches. (Stripes run vertically.) Fringe with fabric strips.

SANGRIAS AT SUNSET

1 Bottle of red wine (Cabernet Sauvignon, Merlot, Rioja, Zinfandel, Shiraz)
1 Lemon cut into wedges
1 Orange cut into wedges
1 Lime cut into wedges
2 Tbsp sugar
Splash of orange juice
2 Shots of gin or triple sec (optional)
1 Cup fresh raspberries
1 Small can of diced pineapple (with juice)
4 Cups diet ginger ale

Pour wine into a large pitcher and squeeze the juice wedges from the lemon, orange and lime into the wine. Toss in the fruit wedges and pineapple then add sugar, orange juice and gin. Chill overnight as you would a marinade. Add ginger ale, berries and ice just before serving.

MATERIALS

One of our most popular kits, Great Balls of Yarn custom coordinates these very special throws into kits to match clients' fabric swatches. This particular model was tailored for one of our best clients. If you wish, simply send us fabric or paint swatches and we can create a breathtaking palette of colors and textures for you. Below are the materials and colorways we used in this specific design.

2 skeins Prism Angora
  (model shown in Arroyo & Spice)
2 skeins Prism Bubble
  (model shown in Garden)
2 skeins Prism Dover
  (model shown in Ginger)
2 skeins Prism Kid Slique
  (model shown in Meadow)
2 skeins Prism Velvet
  (model shown in Ginger)
1 skein Prism Half Inch Ribbon
  (model shown in Ginger)
1 skein Prism Equinox
  (model shown in Freesia)
2 skeins Malabrigo Merino
  Worsted (model shown in
  Deja Vu and Molly)
Optional-Hand-dyed Hanah
Satin-Silk Ribbon custom dyed
to match for fringe

NEEDLE

Size 11 circular
at least 29 inches in length

PARTY GIRL DRESS

MATERIALS

1(1,2,2) skeins Robin Turner
Back to Basics' Prima Pima
(A) model shown in Teal
1(1,1,1) skeins Robin Turner
Back to Basics' Prima Pima
(B) model shown in Plum
1(1,1,1) skeins Robin Turner
Back to Basics' Prima Pima
(C) model shown in Lime

NEEDLES

Size 7

GAUGE

18 sts and 24 rows = 4 inches
in Stockinette worked on size
7 needles

SIZE AND MEASUREMENTS

12 months   Chest 20 ¼ inches
2 years   Chest 23 inches
3 years   Chest 24 ½ inches
4 years   Chest 26 ¼ inches
Length: 15 ½ (18 ¼ , 20 ½ ,23) inches
Lower Hem: 34(38 ½, 40 ½, 44) inches

SEED STITCH

Row 1: *K1, P1; rep from *
Row 2: Knit the purl stitches and purl the knit stitches
Repeat Row 2 for Seed Stitch

STRIPE PATTERN

Work 6 rows A, 4 rows B, 2 rows C – It is recommended to
carry the yarns up the sides, DO NOT CUT

BACK With A, CO 77(87,91,99)sts. ROW 1(RS): K1 *P1,K1;
rep from * to end of row. Rep Row 1 4 times more, end after
RSR. Next row(WS): Purl. This will make 6 rows in A

ESTABLISH STRIPE PATTERN

With B work in stockinette for 4 rows , then with C work in
stockinette for 2 rows. With A work in stockinette for 6 rows.
Repeat this stripe pattern sequence until piece measures 9 ½ (11
½, 13, 14 ½)" from cast on, end after RSR. Next Row (WS):
P1(1,3,2),*P2 TOG, P1, P2 TOG; rep from * to last 1(1,3,2)
sts. P1(1,3,2). 47(53,57,61) sts rem. BO all stitches Knitwise.

BACK BODICE With RS facing and C, pick up and knit
47(53,57,61) stitches along bond off edge. Work in Seed Stitch
maintaining stripe pattern until piece measures 2 ½ (3, 3 ½ , 4)
inches from pick up row, end after WSR. Bind off all stitches
in pattern.

FRONT Work as written for back.

STRAPS (Make 2) with A cast on 7 stitches. Work in Seed
Stitch until piece from cast on measures 7(7 ½, 8, 9) inches (or
desired length). Bind off all stitches in pattern

FINISHING Sew side seams, sew BO and CO edges of strap
to BO edge of Bodice, approx. 1 inch in from each edge.

MINESTRONE & DOLCINO STRIPED JACKET

SIZES AND MEASUREMENTS

Small	Chest Size 33 inches
Medium	Chest Size 36 inches
Large	Chest Size 39 inches
Extra Large	Chest Size 42 inches

Finished size will be 3 inches larger

STITCHES USED

Rib Stitch:
Row 1: *K2,P2*. Rep *to* across the row.
Row 2: Work stitches as set on the needle.
Rev. Stockinette Stitch:
Row 1: (RS) Purl across the row.
Row 2: Knit across the row.
Lace Stitch:
Row 1: (WS) Purl across the row.
Row 2: K1,*Yo,K2TOG*. Rep *to*, end K1.
Row 4: K2,*Yo,K2TOG*. Rep *to* across the row.

BACK With #9 needle and Dolcino, Cast on 72(78,84,90)sts. Work in Rib St. across the row as possible. Continue in pattern for 2". Change to #10 needle and work in patterns as follows: Work 3" Minestrone in Rev. Stock St. (Knit the first RS row so no ridges appear.) Work 3" Lace St. (Change yarn on WS row.) Repeat until 13(13 ½,14,14 ½)" from the cast on. Mark each end and continue in pattern for 7 ½(8,8 ½,9)". Bind off across the next row.

FRONTS With #9 needle and Dolcino, Cast on 36(38,42,44)sts. Work in Rib St. across the row as possible. Continue in pattern for 2". Change to #10 needle and work in patterns as for the back until 5(5 ½,6,6 ½)" above the side marker. Bind off 7sts at the neck edge 1x, then 2sts 1x. Decrease 1 stitch at the neck edge every other row 4x. Continue until 7 ½(8,8 ½,9)" above the marker. Bind off remaining stitches in pattern. Make another front reversing the shaping.

MATERIALS

Trendsetter Yarns
2(3,3,4) balls Minestrone (model shown in Zebra)
6(7,8,9) balls Dolcino (model shown in Black)

NEEDLES
9 and 10

GAUGE
16sts=4 inches with #10 needle and Minestrone in Reverse Stockinette Stitch.

Continued on page 69

SHRUG ME!

MATERIALS

8 (10) balls of Robin Turner
Gourmet Fibers' Deliziosa
(model shown in French Blue)

CROCHET HOOKS

Size F (3.75mm)
Size G (4.0mm) or
  size to obtain gauge.

GAUGE

15 hdc and 11 rows = 4 inches
using larger hook.
Take time to check gauge.

NOTE

Shrug is made all in one
piece with band added after
finishing. It is worked from
left cuff to right cuff. Then
add band. Fronts will not
meet, it is worn Bolero Style.

SIZES

X-Small-Small	Chest Measurement 29 inches
Medium-Large	Chest Measurement 33 inches

DECREASES

HDC2tog: YO, insert hook into next stitch, YO and draw up
a loop (3 loops), YO, draw through 2 loops, (2 loops on hook)
YO, insert hook into next stitch, YO and draw through 2 loops,
YO and draw through all three loops.

DC3tog: YO, insert hook into next stitch, YO and draw
up a loop (3 loops), YO, draw through 2 loops, (2 loops on
hook) YO, insert hook into next stitch (4 loops),YO and draw
through 2 loops, YO and draw through all three loops.

Inc 1: Work 2 stitches in same (one) stitch.

Dec 1: See above.

LEFT SLEEVE

With smaller hook, chain (ch) - 30(43).

Row 1:	(Right Side/RS) Single crochet (sc) in 2nd ch from hook and in each ch across – 38(42) stitches (sts). Ch 1, turn.
Rows 2-4:	Sc in each st across. Ch 1, turn. *Change to larger hook, Ch 2, turn.
Row 5:	Hdc across increasing 6(8) evenly spaced – 44(50) Hdc, Ch 2, turn.
Rows 6-8:	Hdc in each st across. Ch2, turn.
Row 9:	Work 2 hdc in first st, hdc in each st to last st, work 2 hdc in last st (46(52) hdc, Ch 2, turn.
Row 10- 12:	Hdc in each hdc across, Ch 2, turn.
Row 13-28:	Repeat Row 9 – 12 four more times – 54(60) hdc. Ch 2, turn
Rows 29 & 30:	Repeat Row 9 twice more – 58(64 hdc. Ch 2, turn.

Continued on page 69

Play

LITTLE BELLE BLUE

MATERIALS
5 (6, 7) balls **Robin Turner Gourmet Fibers**' Deliziosa (model shown in Baby Blue)

NEEDLES
Size 6

GAUGE
22 sts and 30 rows = 4 inches in pattern stitch

EVERYONE'S HAPPY HOUR SPINACH & ARTICHOKE DIP

1 (8 ounce) package
   cream cheese, softened
1/4 cup mayonnaise
1/4 cup grated Parmesan cheese
1/4 cup grated Romano cheese
1 clove garlic, peeled and minced
1/2 teaspoon dried basil
1/4 teaspoon garlic salt
Salt and pepper to taste
1 (14 ounce) can artichoke hearts,
   drained and chopped
1/2 cup frozen chopped spinach,
   thawed and drained
1/4 cup shredded mozzarella cheese
Light Triscuits or your cracker of choice

FINISHED CHEST MEASUREMENT
Small   38 inches
Medium   42 inches
Large   46 inches

PATTERN SEQUENCE
Row 1: (RS) K1 *Knit, wrapping yarn twice around needles for each stitch*, K1.
Row 2: (WS) K1 and drop extra wrap for each stitch, K1, *P3TOG, YO, P3TOG in next 3 sts. Repeat from * to last st, K1.
Row 3: (RS) Knit
Row 4: (WS) Knit
Row 5: (RS) Repeat Row 1.
Row 6: (WS) K1 and drop extra wrap for each stitch across row, K1.
Row 7: (RS) Knit
Row 8: (WS) Knit

MAKE TWO IDENTICAL PIECES.
With Size 6 needle, CO 101 (116, 131) sts. Begin working in pattern sequence until piece measures 19 (20, 21) inches or until length desired, finishing after either Row 4 or Row 8. Knit two more additional rows then BO all stitches.

FINISHING
Sew shoulders together leaving approximately 12 to 12 ½ inches in middle for neck opening. Sew sides leaving 7 ½ (8, 9) inches for armhole openings. Weave in ends and gently block.

Preheat oven to 350 degrees. Lightly grease a small baking dish.
In a medium bowl, mix together cream cheese, mayonnaise, Parmesan cheese, Romano cheese, garlic, basil, garlic salt, salt and pepper. Gently stir in artichoke hearts and spinach. Transfer the mixture to the prepared baking dish. Top with mozzarella cheese. Bake in the preheated oven 25 minutes, until bubbly and lightly browned. Serve with crackers, olives and your favorite accoutrements.

WELLINGTON POLO PULLOVER

FINISHED CHEST MEASUREMENT

Small	34 inches
Medium	38 inches
Large	42 inches
Extra Large	46 inches

PATTERN STITCH

Row 1 (WS): With (B), *insert right needle into next st as though to knit, wrap yarn around both needles, wrap yarn around back needle only, then pull through both loops as if to knit regularly, creating a modified drop stitch. Repeat from * to end.

Row 2 (RS): With (B), knit across row.

Row 3 (WS): With (A), knit across row.

Row 4 (RS): With (A), knit across row.

Row 5 (WS): With (A), purl across row.

Row 6 (RS): With (A), knit across row.

Row 7 (WS): Repeat Row 5.

Row 8 (RS): Repeat Row 6.

These 8 rows form pattern.

BACK AND FRONT (Make Alike)

With size 6 needles, and (A) CO 94 (104, 114, 124) sts. Row 1(WS): Knit. Join in (B). Starting with a knit row, work in stockinette using (A) for 7 rows, ending after a RS row. Begin to work in pattern. Continue to work in pattern until work measures 13(13 ¼, 13 ¾, 14 ¼) inches from CO edge and ending on a WS row.

BEGIN ARMHOLE SHAPING

Keeping in pattern, BO 5 sts loosely at the beg of next 2 rows. 84 (94, 104, 114) sts. Dec 1 sts at each end of next and following 4 alt rows. 74 (84, 94, 104) sts. Work even until armhole measures 8 ¼(8 ½, 9, 9 ¼) inches, ending after a WS row.

Continued on page 70

MATERIALS

3(3, 3, 4) skeins **Robin Turner Gourmet Fibers'** Soft Dreams (A) (model shown in Mulberry)
3(3, 3, 4) skeins Koigu KPPPM to match (B)

NEEDLES

Size 6

GAUGE

20 sts and 16 rows = 4 inches in stockinette stitch

SMOKED SALMON CANAPES

3 tablespoons light cream cheese
1/2 tablespoon Dijon mustard
3 tablespoons chopped fresh chives
Melba Toast crackers
6 ounces thinly sliced
   smoked salmon

Mix light cream cheese, Dijon mustard and 1 1/2 tablespoons chives in small bowl. Spread scant 1 teaspoon mixture over each toast cracker. Divide smoked salmon among toast crackers. Cut each bread slice into 4 equal triangles. Sprinkle salmon on bread with remaining 1 1/2 tablespoons chives and ground pepper. Garnish with remaining chives

CHICKEN MAC & CHEESE CASSEROLE

1 pound skinless, boneless,
    chicken breast halves
1 to 2 teaspoon dried Italian
    seasoning, crushed
Salt and ground black pepper
1 tablespoon olive oil
8 ounces dried mostaccioli pasta
    or elbows
1 medium onion, chopped (1/2 cup)
2 cloves garlic, minced
3 tablespoons butter
3 tablespoons all-purpose flour
3 cups milk
8 ounces smoked cheddar, Gruyere,
    or Swiss cheese, shredded (2 cups)
Salt and ground black pepper
2 cups soft sourdough or
    French bread crumbs
2 ounces finely shredded Parmesan
    or Romano cheese (1/2 cup)
3 tablespoons butter, melted

Preheat oven to 350 degree F. Cut chicken into
bite-sized pieces. In a large skillet cook chicken,
browning slightly with Italian or desired seasoning
blend, salt, and pepper in hot oil over medium heat
until chicken is no longer pink. Remove chicken
from skillet; set aside.   In a large pot cook pasta
according to package directions until just tender.
Drain; return pasta to pot. Meanwhile, in the same
skillet in which chicken was cooked, cook onion
and garlic in 3 tablespoons hot butter over medium
heat until tender. Stir in flour until well combined.
Stir in tomato paste. Add milk. Cook and stir until
mixture is thickened and bubbly; reduce heat. Add
the shredded cheese. Stir until cheese is almost
melted. Remove from heat. Season to taste with
salt and pepper. Add sauce and chicken to cooked
pasta in pot; stir to coat. Spoon mixture into a 2-
quart square or rectangular baking dish. In a small
bowl stir together bread crumbs, Parmesan cheese,
and 3 tablespoons melted butter. Sprinkle crumb
mixture over pasta mixture. Bake, uncovered, for
20 to 25 minutes or until crumb is browned.

BAKED AUBERGINES

4 small aubergines (or one per serving)
4 large tomatoes, peeled and chopped
2 cups crumbled mozzarella cheese
2 tablespoons (30 ml) olive oil
2 or 3 leaves of fresh basil, finely chopped
   (or ½ teaspoon dried)
1 teaspoon sugar
Salt and pepper
More olive oil to bake the aubergines
Grated parmesan cheese

Slice aubergine into ¼ inch thick slices length-wise, keeping stem at top. Fan open and place on a lightly oiled baking tray and sprinkle with salt. Leave for about an hour to let the bitter juices drain off. Rinse the aubergines and wipe dry. Bake at 400 degrees until lightly browned and softed, about 20 minutes depending on size. Heat 2 tablespoons (30 ml) olive oil, add the diced tomatoes, basil, salt and pepper and cook until the tomatoes have formed a thick sauce-like consistency. When aubergines have cooked through, place on hot plate, fanning the aubergine open. Spread hot tomato sauce on top, Sprinkle on cheese and garnish with fresh basil.

Gourmet

TIMELESS HOURGLASS TANK

FINISHED CHEST MEASUREMENT

Extra Small   32 inches
Small   34 inches
Medium   36 inches
Large   38 inches
Extra Large   40 inches

BACK

With size 7 needles, CO 80 (84, 92, 96, 100) sts. Work in 2 x 2 rib for two inches. Continue in stockinette stitch until piece measures 5 inches from CO edge.

HOURGLASS SHAPING

Dec 1 st each side every 4th row 3 times. Work even for another 7 rows, completing a WS row. Increase 1 st each side every 4th row 3 times. 80 (84, 92, 96, 100) sts. Continue to work even in stockinette stitch until piece measures 15 inches or desired length to armhole.

ARMHOLE SHAPING

BO 3 (4, 5, 6, 6) sts at beg of next 2 rows 74 (76, 82, 84, 88) sts. Dec 1 st each side, every other row 3 (4, 5, 6, 6) times. 68 (68, 72, 72, 76) sts remain on needle. Continue in pattern stitch until piece measures 23 (23 ½ , 23 ½, 24, 24) inches from CO edge.

SHOULDING SHAPING

Place 11 sts from each shoulder onto 2 sep holders. Place center 46 (46, 50, 50, 54) sts on another holder. Work to center 14 (14, 18, 18, 22) sts, attach a second ball of yarn, BO center 14 (15, 16, 16, 16) st then complete remainder of row in pattern stitch. 27 stitches will remain on each side. Working both sides at once, Dec 1 st at each neck edge, every row 16 (16, 16, 16, 16) times. Continue in pattern stitch until piece measures 23 (24, 24, 25, 25) inches from CO edge.

Continued on page 70

MATERIALS
3 (3, 3, 4, 4) skeins **Robin Turner Back to Basics'** Prima Pima (model shown in Fuchsia)

NEEDLES
Size 7 straight
One 16 inch size 7 circular

GAUGE
5 sts = 1 inch in stockinette stitch

JERSEY FAIR BLUEBERRY MUFFINS

½ cup unsalted butter, softened
1 cup sugar
2 large eggs
1 teaspoon vanilla
2 teaspoons baking powder
¼ teaspoon salt
2 ½ cups fresh blueberry
2 cups sifted flour
½ cup milk

For Topping
1 tablespoon sugar, mixed with
¼ teaspoon ground nutmeg

Preheat oven to 375°. Grease 18 regular-size muffin cups (or 12 large size muffins). In bowl, mix butter until creamy. Add sugar and beat until fluffy. Add eggs, beating after each. Beat in vanilla, baking powder and salt. Fold in flour and milk into batter with a large mixing spoon. Fold in blueberries. Spoon into muffin cups and sprinkle topping onto each muffin. Bake 20 to 30 minutes, until golden brown and springy to touch.

ORKNEY VEST

MATERIALS
9 (10, 10, 11, 11, 12) balls
Naturally Vero (chunky weight), 87 yarns/50 grams
8 (9, 9, 10, 11, 12) balls
Trendsetter Tonalita (worsted weight), 100 yards/50 grams
Buttons: 3 (or 4) buttons at least 1 inch in diameter

NEEDLES
Size 10 (or size required to achieve gauge) and size 9 (or one size smaller than main needle).
Size 9 (or size required to achieve gauge) and size 8 (or one size smaller than main needle).
Size I crochet hook
Size H crochet hook

FINISHED MEASUREMENTS:
Approximately 36 (40, 44, 48, 52, 56) inches
Gauge: 3.5 sts per inch in garter ridge stitch
4.5 sts per inch in garter ridge stitch

PATTERN STITCH
Garter Ridge Stitch -- K 3 rows, P 1 row.
Abbreviations:
K Knit
P Purl
RS Right side
WS Wrong side
St(s) Stitch or stitches
Decr Decrease
K2 tog Knit two sts together (a decrease)
SSK slip st as if to knit, slip st as if to knit, k sl sts tog
Sl Slip as if to purl
Ch Chain

DESIGNER NOTES
This garment employs a simple selvage on the back pieces that makes picking up stitches and sewing much easier. To do this, knit the first stitch of every row, WS and RS, through the back loop, and slip the last stitch of every row, WS and RS, as if to purl. I have manipulated colors considerably, choosing to 'anchor' the cap sleeves in a single color, and to do the same with the starting colors for many of the triangles. Manipulation may require purchase of an additional ball of yarn. But it lends coherence to the finished garment. We show three buttons; you could easily use four, adding a final button and button hole at the very bottom. We think a loose bottom edge is more flattering for most women.

MATERIALS
9 (9, 10) Balls Robin Turner
Back to Basics' Microwash
Model shown in Cranberry

NEEDLES
Size 8
Cable needle

GAUGE
4 sts and 6 rows = 1 inch in
stockinette with size 8 needle

THE CHESTERFIELD COSMOPOLITAN

3 parts Grey Goose L'Orange Vodka
1 part Cointreau
1-2 parts cranberry juice
Splash of Rose's Lime juice
1 designated driver

Add all ingredients into a cocktail
shaker filled with ice. Shake well
and strain into a large cocktail glass.
Garnish with an orange slice. Hard
to have just one!

WORTH AVENUE WALKABOUT SWEATER

Pair it with some sexy stovepipe jeans, or belt it with a pair of
classic slacks…Either way, you'll look like you just stepped off
Worth Avenue in this designer-look sweater with contrasting
moss-stitch and wide cables at the neckline. Make one in every
color to fit your every mood!

SIZES
Small	Bust 32 to 34 inches
Medium	Bust 36 to 38 inches
Large	Bust 40 to 42 inches

PATTERN STITCHES
Three by One Rib
Row 1: Knit 3, P1 to last 3 stitches, end Knit 3
Row 2: Purl 3, Knit 1 to last 3 stitches, end Purl 3
Double Moss Stitch
Row 1: K1, K2, P2, across, end K1
       (keep first and last st in stockinette)
Row 2: P1, P2, K2 across, end P1.
Row 3: K1, P2, PK2 across, end K1.
Row 4: P1, K2, P2 across, end P1.

CABLE PATTERN
Row 1, 3, 5, 7, 9 13, 15, 17, 19, 21: P10, K 12, P 11, K 12, P
11, K 12, P 10
Row 2, 4, 6, 8, 10, 12, 1, 16, 18, 20: K 10, P 12, K 11, P 12, K
11, P 12, K 10.
Row 11: P 10, * sl next 3 sts to cable needle and hold n back, K
3, then K 3 from cable needle, sl 3 sts to cable needle and hold in
front, K 3, knit 3 fron cable needle, P 11, repeat from *, end P 10.

BODY (make two)
Cast on 75 (79, 83 stitches. Work 3X1 Rib, dec 1 st. on last row
(74, 78 82 sts). Work Double Moss Pattern until piece measures
13 inches. Mark edge stitch with marker. Continue in Double
Moss Pattern for 3 more inches. Start cable pattern
Contine Double Moss stitch 8 more rows, bind off in pattern.

Continued on page 71

MINTED TABBOULEH SALAD

1 cup bulgur wheat
3 tomatoes, seeded and chopped
2 cucumbers, peeled and chopped
3 green onions, chopped
3 cloves garlic, minced
1 ½ cup chopped fresh parsley
½ cup fresh mint leaves
2 teaspoons salt
½ cup lemon juice
¾ cup olive oil

Place cracked wheat in bowl and cover with 2 cups boiling water. Soak for 30 minutes; drain and squeeze out excess water.
In a mixing bowl, combine the wheat, tomatoes, cucumbers, onions, garlic, parsley, mint, salt, lemon juice, and olive oil. Toss and refrigerate for at least 4 hours before serving. Toss again prior to serving.

CLASSIC RACK OF LAMB

1 two-pound rack of lamb
2 tablespoons extra-virgin olive oil
Salt and freshly ground black pepper
1/2 cup minced fresh parsley leaves
1 teaspoon Herbs de Provence
1 teaspoon minced garlic
1 tablespoon sugar
Mint Jelly to Garnish
Fresh Coriander to Garnish

Pre-heat the oven to 475° F. Trim the lamb of excess fat, but leave a layer of fat over the meat. Cut about half-way down the bones between the chops; this allows the meat between them to become crisp. (Frenching.) Combine the oil, parsley, herbs, and garlic and rub over the meat side of the racks. Sprinkle the racks with the sugar along with salt and pepper. Roast for 20 minutes and insert an instant-read meat thermometer straight in from one end into the meatiest part. If it reads 125° F or more, remove the lamb immediately. If it reads less, put the lamb back for 5 minutes, no more. Remove and let sit for 5 minutes. Serve by separating the ribs by cutting down straight through them. Garnish with coriander and mint jelly.

Patterns Continued

SWEET DREAMS
Continue from page 8

BACK
With size 7 needles, and (A) CO 55 (60, 65, 70) sts then with (B) CO 35 (40, 45, 50) sts for a total of 90 (100, 110, 120) sts. Row 1(WS): With (B) K35 (40, 45, 50) with (A) K55 (60, 65, 70. Changing color in the same place on each row, work two more rows in garter stitch. Change to stockinette stitch. While changing color in the same place on each row, work even until piece measures 19 (19 ½ , 20, 20 ½) inches from CO edge.

BEGIN ARMHOLE SHAPING
BO 0 (4, 5, 7) sts at beg of next 2 rows. Next row (decrease row): K1, SSK, K to last 3 sts, changing color as established, K2TOG, K1. Next row (WS): Purl. Continue in stockinette, working the decrease row on every RS row 26 (27, 30, 32) times more—36 (36, 38, 40) sts remain. BO loosely.

FRONT
With size 7 needles, and (B) CO 55 (60, 65, 70) sts then with (A) CO 35 (40, 45, 50) sts for a total of 90 (100, 110, 120) sts. Row 1(WS): With (A) K35 (40, 45, 50) with (B) K55 (60, 65, 70. Work the same as the back, including armhole shaping until 50 (50, 52, 54) sts remain, ending with the RS facing for the next row.

BEGIN SHAPING FRONT NECK
Next row (RS): K1, SSK, K8, K2TOG, K1, then join a second ball of yarn and BO the center 22 (22, 24, 26) sts, K1, SSK, K2TOG, K1. Continue working in stockinette, decreasing 1 st on each side at both armhole edge and center front edge until 2 sts remain on each side. Bind off.

SLEEVES
Work right sleeve with color (A). Work left sleeve with color (B). With size 7 needle, CO 60 (60, 65, 70 sts. Knit 3 rows. Change to stockinette and increase 1 st at the beginning and the end of every 10th row 0 (5, 5, 5) times—60 (70, 75, 80) sts. Continue without shaping until the sleeve measures 18 inches or desired length to armhole, ending with the RS facing for the next row.

BEGIN SLEEVE SHAPING
Bind off 0 (4, 5, 7) sts at the beginning of the next 2 rows. Decrease 1 st at the beginning and the end of the next row, then every 4th row 3 (3, 5, 7) times, then every other row 20 (21, 20, 19) times. BO remaining 12 (12, 13, 12) sts.

FINISHING
Sew sleeves to front and back of each raglan line.

MAKE I-CORDS
With circular needle, and Prima Pima, CO 3 sts. *Knit 3. Slide the sts to the opposite end of the needle, pull the working yarn around the back of the sts and repeat from *. Work until desired length. Bind off. Make 2 cords that are 26 inches in length and made 2 additional cords that are 5 inches long.

With color (A) sew the decorative I-Cord down both color joins on the front and back. Sew the smaller cords to the cuff of each sleeve.

NECKLINE FINISHING
With the circular needle and Prima Pima, pick up and knit 99 (99, 103, 107) sts around the perimeter of the neck, making sure to work through the upper edge of the front and back I-cords. Join to work in the round. Knit 6 rounds the BO loosely. Fold neck band to the inside to create a mock I-cord and sew to attach.

Block lightly.

MAY DAY RUFFLED SUNTOP
Continue from page 10

BODY
Three ruffles joined. Piece measures 6 (7 ½, 9, 10 ½) inches from cast on of bottom ruffle.

DIVIDING ROW
Continue with smaller needle and color C. Bind off 6 (8, 10, 12) sts for left underarm, K 40 (41, 42, 43) front stitches, bind off 6 (8, 10, 12) sts for right underarm, knit to end (40, 41, 42, 43) stitches. (These are your back stitches) Turn, leaving front sts on the needle and begin working back and forth in rows on back stitches only.

BACK
Next row: (WS) continue in stockinette, work 1 purl row even.

YARN RESOURCES

PRISM Galaxy
95% Nylon, 5% Metallic Polyester
This fanciful wide ribbon with
metallic accents creates a beautiful
trim or fringe.
[6] SUPER BULKY 54 yards per skein

PRISM Kid Slique
66% Rayon, 26% Kid Mohair,
8% Nylon
Two strands of different fibers take
the hand-dyes in a wonderfully lumi
nous juxtaposition of color. A classic
yet sophisticated Prism specialty yarn.
[4] MEDIUM 88 yards per skein

PRISM Velvet
100% Nylon
A ribbon with one soft plush, chenille
edge, another unusual hand-dye
Prism yarn.
[4] MEDIUM 88 yards per skein

**ROBIN TURNER BACK TO
BASICS' Prima Pima**
100% Pima Cotton
An endearing classic, super soft with a
non-pilling construction.
[3] LIGHT 218 yards per skein

**ROBIN TURNER BACK TO
BASICS' MicroWash**
100% Microfibre
Machine washable, dryer friendly.
These attributes make MicroWash a
popular staple for garments and décor
for the entire family.
[4] MEDIUM 87 yards per ball

**ROBIN TURNER GOURMET
FIBERS' Bolivian Alpaca**
100% De-haired Royal Alpaca
A Great Balls of Yarn favorite,
super soft, lighter and warmer
than cashmere.
[3] LIGHT 220 yards per skein

**ROBIN TURNER GOURMET
FIBERS' Deliziosa**
100% Extrafine Superwash
Lana Merino
Made in Italy exclusively for
Great Balls of Yarn. The spin and
color range of this irresistible merino
make it a popular choice for a myriad
of projects.
[3] LIGHT 155 yards per ball

**ROBIN TURNER GOURMET
FIBERS' Heavenly Angora**
80% Angora 10% Lana Wool
10% Nylon
Super soft angora in lovely colors with
a touch of wool and nylon for stability.
[3] LIGHT 165 yards per skein

**ROBIN TURNER GOURMET
FIBERS' Potpourri with Paillettes**
Various compositions and blends of
yarns with large paillettes stranded
throughout a menagerie of color,
texture and sparkle, Potpourri with
Paillettes is made in small batches that
cannot be replicated.
[5] BULKY 200 yards per skein

**ROBIN TURNER GOURMET
FIBERS' Silky Llama**
Baby Llama 70% Mulberry Silk 30%
The highest quality silk spun with
luxurious de-haired baby llama.
[3] LIGHT 218 yards per skein

**ROBIN TURNER GOURMET
FIBERS' Soft Dreams**
70% Extra Fine Kid Mohair 30% Silk
A lofty and luminous fine mohair
that's gentle to the touch. A suitable
choice for fine lace work yet also
durable for sweater patterning.
[2] FINE 230 yards ber ball

TRENDSETTER Cha Cha
47% Wool, 47% Acrylic, 6% Nylon
A versatile trim, knitting through
top edge of each open box creates
delicate ruffles, or one can simply knit
with this wide ribbon, yielding
a Berber effect.
[6] SUPER BULKY 65 yards per skein.

TRENDSETTER Dolcino
75% Acrylic/25% Nylon
Imported from Italy, this soft and
pliable ribbon lends itself to virtually
any couture project. A plethora of
colors which correspond to the entire
Trendsetter line.
[5] BULKY 100 yards per skein

TRENDSETTER Minestrone
75% Polyamide, 24% Acrylic,
1% Polyester Metalic
A glamorous, multi-textured yarn,
Minestrone lends itself to many uses
and is dyed to match other popular
Trendsetter novelty yarns and
self-ruffling varieties.
[5] BULKY 110 yards per skein

TRENDSETTER Tonalita
52% Wool, 48% Acrylic
Subtle color changes, terrific self-strip-
ing, and superbly soft, a fabulous yarn
that is dyed to match one of our very
favorite yarns, Trendsetter Dune.
[4] MEDIUM 100 yards per ball

Patterns Continued

SWEET DREAMS
Continue from page 8

BACK
With size 7 needles, and (A) CO 55 (60, 65, 70) sts then with (B) CO 35 (40, 45, 50) sts for a total of 90 (100, 110, 120) sts. Row 1(WS): With (B) K35 (40, 45, 50) with (A) K55 (60, 65, 70. Changing color in the same place on each row, work two more rows in garter stitch. Change to stockinette stitch. While changing color in the same place on each row, work even until piece measures 19 (19 ½ , 20, 20 ½) inches from CO edge.

BEGIN ARMHOLE SHAPING
BO 0 (4, 5, 7) sts at beg of next 2 rows. Next row (decrease row): K1, SSK, K to last 3 sts, changing color as established, K2TOG, K1. Next row (WS): Purl. Continue in stockinette, working the decrease row on every RS row 26 (27, 30, 32) times more—36 (36, 38, 40) sts remain. BO loosely.

FRONT
With size 7 needles, and (B) CO 55 (60, 65, 70) sts then with (A) CO 35 (40, 45, 50) sts for a total of 90 (100, 110, 120) sts. Row 1(WS): With (A) K35 (40, 45, 50) with (B) K55 (60, 65, 70. Work the same as the back, including armhole shaping until 50 (50, 52, 54) sts remain, ending with the RS facing for the next row.

BEGIN SHAPING FRONT NECK
Next row (RS): K1, SSK, K8, K2TOG, K1, then join a second ball of yarn and BO the center 22 (22, 24, 26) sts, K1, SSK, K2TOG, K1. Continue working in stockinette, decreasing 1 st on each side at both armhole edge and center front edge until 2 sts remain on each side. Bind off.

SLEEVES
Work right sleeve with color (A). Work left sleeve with color (B). With size 7 needle, CO 60 (60, 65, 70 sts. Knit 3 rows. Change to stockinette and increase 1 st at the beginning and the end of every 10th row 0 (5, 5, 5) times—60 (70, 75, 80) sts. Continue without shaping until the sleeve measures 18 inches or desired length to armhole, ending with the RS facing for the next row.

BEGIN SLEEVE SHAPING
Bind off 0 (4, 5, 7) sts at the beginning of the next 2 rows. Decrease 1 st at the beginning and the end of the next row, then every 4th row 3 (3, 5, 7) times, then every other row 20 (21, 20, 19) times. BO remaining 12 (12, 13, 12) sts.

FINISHING
Sew sleeves to front and back of each raglan line.

MAKE I-CORDS
With circular needle, and Prima Pima, CO 3 sts. *Knit 3. Slide the sts to the opposite end of the needle, pull the working yarn around the back of the sts and repeat from *. Work until desired length. Bind off. Make 2 cords that are 26 inches in length and made 2 additional cords that are 5 inches long.

With color (A) sew the decorative I-Cord down both color joins on the front and back. Sew the smaller cords to the cuff of each sleeve.

NECKLINE FINISHING
With the circular needle and Prima Pima, pick up and knit 99 (99, 103, 107) sts around the perimeter of the neck, making sure to work through the upper edge of the front and back I-cords. Join to work in the round. Knit 6 rounds the BO loosely. Fold neck band to the inside to create a mock I-cord and sew to attach.

Block lightly.

MAY DAY RUFFLED SUNTOP
Continue from page 10

BODY
Three ruffles joined. Piece measures 6 (7 ½, 9, 10 ½) inches from cast on of bottom ruffle.

DIVIDING ROW
Continue with smaller needle and color C. Bind off 6 (8, 10, 12) sts for left underarm, K 40 (41, 42, 43) front stitches, bind off 6 (8, 10, 12) sts for right underarm, knit to end (40, 41, 42, 43) stitches. (These are your back stitches) Turn, leaving front sts on the needle and begin working back and forth in rows on back stitches only.

BACK
Next row: (WS) continue in stockinette, work 1 purl row even.

Patterns Continued

SHAPE ARMHOLES

Next row: (RS) (Knit row) Bind off 2 sts at the beginning of the next 2 rows, then bind off 0 (1, 1, 2) sts at the beginning of the next 2 rows 36 (35, 36, 35) sts remain. Next row: (RS) At each armhole edge, decrease 1 stitch every other row 3 (3, 3, 3) times 30, (29, 30, 29) sts remain. Work even until piece measures 1 ½, 2, 2 ½, 3) inches from the dividing row, end after WS row. Change to garter st and work 4 rows even.

SHAPE NECK AND STRAPS

Next row (RS): K5, bind off center 20 (19, 20, 19) sts., knit to end (5 sts each side for straps). Working one strap at a time, work in garter st. until strap measures 3 inches from neck bind off.

BUTTONHOLE ROW

Next row: (RS) K1, K2 tog, YO, K2, Knit one row, working YO as a stitch. Shape strap: Next row (WS): K2TOG, K1 K2TOG, turn, (3 sts remain). Sl 1, K2TOG, psso. Fasten off. Repeat for other strap.

FRONT

Work as for back until piece measures 1 (1 ½, 2, 2 ½) inches from dividing row. End after WS row. Change to garter st work 4 rows even. BO all sts.

FINISHING

Optional edging – using a crochet hook, join C and work 1 row single crochet evenly around neck and arm¬hole edges. Fasten off. Sew buttons on front, opposite buttonholes.

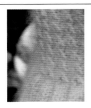

GORGEOUS, LUSCIOUS MOCK CABLE SHRUG
Continue from page 15

INCREASE NOTE

The following increases are worked in K sts only by tipping left needle forward knitting into the purl bump on the stitch below the one on the needle, then knitting into the st on the needle. Increases are made in the next 2 rows. The increases at the beg and end of row are worked by knitting into the front and back of the stitch because it is awkward to knit into purl bumps of sts on edge of work.

Row 1 (RS): K in front & back of 1st st, *P2, inc in next 2 K sts by knitting into purl bumps.* Repeat from between * to first marker, slip marker, K1, inc in back of next st in purl bump, K1, P2* to 3 sts before next marker, K1, inc in next st, K1, slip marker, *P2, inc in next 2 K sts, to 3 sts before end, P2, K in back and front of last sts.

Row 2 (WS): P2*, inc by working into purl bumps of next 2 K sts, P4.* Repeat between to last 4 sts, inc in next 2 K sts, P2,

Next Row: Change to larger needle and cont in K4, P4 ribbing for 7 (8, 9) inches.

Bind off loosely using tip of # 9 needle.

FINISHING

Fold garment in half so the cast on edge and bound off edge are together. Sew side seams to where pattern

JUDE'S ENTRELAC BLANKET
Continue from page 25

3rd and 4th rows set pattern. Repeat Rows 3 and 4 six more times then work 3rd row once more.

Next Row
*Pick up and purl 11 sts evenly down left side of diamond, working across these 12 sts and next 12 sts on left hand needle proceed as follows: Turn; K12, turn; P2TOG, P9, P2TOG, turn, K11, turn; P2TOG, P8, P2TOG, turn; K10, turn; P2TOG, turn; P7, P2TOG, turn; K9, turn; P2TOG, P6, P2TOG, turn; K8, turn; P2TOG, P5, P2TOG, turn; K7, turn; P2TOG, P4, P2TOG, turn; K6, turn; P2TOG, P3, P2TOG, turn; K5, turn; P2TOG, P2, P2TOG, K4, turn; P2TOG, P1, P2TOG, turn; K3, turn; P2TOG twice, turn; K2, turn; P4TOG, rep from * to end.

BORDER

Top and bottom border are alike: With smaller needles and RS facing pickup and knit 148 sts evenly along short edge.
Row 1: K1, P2, *K2, P2, rep from * to last st, K1.
Row 2: P1, *K2, P2, rep from * to last 3 sts, K2, P1.
Rows 1 and 2 set rib pattern
Work 11 rows more in rib ending with a WS row.
Cast off in rib.

SIDE BORDERS

With smaller needles and RS facing using pick up and knit 12 sts evenly along 1st border, 186 sts evenly along long edge and 12 sts evenly along 2nd border for a total of 210 sts.
Row 1: P2, *K2, P2, rep from *to end.
Row 2: K2, P2, rep from * to last 2 sts, K2
Work 11 rows more in rib ending with a WS row. Cast off in rib.

FINISHING

Weave in all ends, lightly block with damp cloth. Find a coordinating receiving blanket and sew to WS of blanket for a clean finish.

ALPACA CABLE SWEATER

Continue from page 26

BODY

CO 66(66,66,72,78,78) sts at END of next 2 rows for Back & Right Front. 228(228,228,256,276,276) sts. Continue in Cable pattern on sleeve, work inc. sts (Back and Front) in St st until next (WS) Row 10 of Cable Pattern has been worked.
Re-Establish Cable Pattern
Next row (RS): Beginning at lower edge of Right Front, K8(8,8,4,8,8), pm; work Row 1 of Cable pattern across to last 4(4,4,12,4,4)sts of Back, C8F0(0,0,1,0,0) times, pm, K4. Keeping sts between markers in Cable pattern, rem sts in St st, work even until Right Front measures 5 ½(6 ¼, 7 ¼,8, 8 ¾,9 ½) inches from CO, end after WS row.

SHAPE NECK

Next Row (RS): BO 114(114,114,128,138,138) Right Front sts; pattern to end. 114(114,114,128,138,138 stitches remain for Back. Work even in pattern until Back (neck edge) measures 6(6 ½,6 ½,7, 7 ½,8) inches from Right Front BO, end after WS row. DO NOT TURN and CO 114(114,114,128,138,138) stitches at end of row for Left Front, turn work. 228(228,228,256,276,276) sts total on needle.
Re-Establish Cable Pattern
Next Row (RS): Beginning at lower edge of Left Front, re-establish Cable pattern as for Right Front (above). Work even until Left Front measures 5 ½,(6 ¼,7 ¼,8, 8 ¾,9 ½) nches from CO, end after WS row.
Next Row (RS): BO 66(66,66,72,78,78) sts at beginning of next 2 rows for Left Front and Back. 96(96,96,112.120,120) sts remain.

LEFT SLEEVE

Continue in pattern, work even until Sleeve measures 1(1,1,2,2 ½, 2 ½,) inches from last BO row, end after RS row. Next row (WS): continue in pattern, dec 24(24,24,28,30,30) sts evenly across next row as follows: *P2, P2TOG; rep from*across 72(72,72,84,90,90) sts remain. Next Row (RS): Change to 3 x 3 rib; work even until Sleeve measures 4(4,4,5,5 ½,5 ½) inches from last BO row, rib is 3 inches end after WS row, BO all sts loosely in rib.

FINISHING

Sew sleeve and side seams

FRONT BANDS

With RS facing, beg at lower hem edge of Right Front, pick up and knit 90(90,90,96,102,102) sts up Front to neck edge. Next row (WS): Beg 3 x 3 rib; work even until band measures 3(3 ¼, 3 ¼,3 ½,3 ¾,4) inches from pick up row end after WS row. BO all sts loosely in rib. With RS facing, beginning at Left Front neck edge, work as for Right Front band.

COLLAR

With RS facing, pick up and knit 15(17,17,21,22,24) sts along upper edge of Right Front band, pick up and knit 36(38,38,38,42,46,48) sts across Back neck, pick up and knit 15(17,17,21,22,24)sts along upper edge of Left Front band.. 66(72,72,84,90,96)sts. Next row (WS): Beginning 3 x 3 rib; work even until Collar measures 7(7,7,71/2,8,8) inches from pick up row, end after WSR. BO all sts loosely in rib.

WAVE STITCH PULLOVER

Continue from page 31

Repeat rows 1-12

Chart Symbols:
K1 on both Right Side a
nd Wrong Side
[3] YO 3 times, K1
[1] YO, K1
[4] YO 4 times, K1
[2] YO twice, K1
•knit, dropping all YO's off needle

Continued on page 68

Patterns Continued

FRONT/BACK

CO 92 (102, 108) sts. Work in Wave Stitch Pattern (according to Chart or Alternate Chart Written Instruction) for 13 3/8 (14, 15)", positioning pattern as foll:

• For chest 34-36 - selvage stitch, 9 last sts of Wave Stitch Pattern, then work 24-stitch pattern repeat 3 times, finish row with 9 first sts of Wave Stitch Pattern and selvage stitch.

•For chest 38 - selvage stitch, 2 last sts of Wave Stitch Pattern, then work 24-stitch pattern repeat 4 times, finish row with 2 first sts of Wave Stitch Pattern and selvage stitch

• For chest 40 - selvage stitch, 5 last sts of Wave Stitch Pattern, then work 24-stitch pattern repeat 4 times, finish row with 5 first sts of Wave Stitch Pattern and selvage stitch.

Shape armholes: bind off 9 (10, 12) sts at beg of next 2 rows =74 (82, 84) sts. Continue working remaining sts in Wave Stitch Pattern until piece measures 201/2 (211/2, 223/4)" from CO, as foll:

• For chest 34-36 - selvage stitch, work 24-stitch pattern repeat 3 times, selvage stitch.

• For chest 38 - selvage stitch, 4 last sts of Wave Stitch Pattern, then work 24-stitch pattern repeat 3 times, finish row with 4 first sts of Wave Stitch Pattern and selvage stitch

• For chest 40 - selvage stitch, 5 last sts of Wave Stitch Pattern, then work 24-stitch pattern repeat 3 times, finish row with 5 first sts of Wave Stitch Pattern and selvage stitch.

Work in Garter Stitch (knit every row) for approx. ¾ (1, 1)" more until piece measures 211/4 (221/2, 233/4)" from CO. Loosely bind off all stitches.

SLEEVES

CO 50 (50, 54) sts. and work in Wave Stitch Pattern, positioning pattern as foll:

• For chest 34-36 & 38 - selvage stitch, work 24-Wave-stitch pattern repeat 2 times, selvage stitch.

• For chest 40 - selvage stitch, 2 last sts of Wave Stitch Pattern, then work 24-stitch pattern repeat 2 times, finish row with 2 first sts of Wave Stitch Pattern and selvage stitch

When piece measures 43/8", increase:

• For chest 34-36 - 1 st at beg and end of next row. Repeat this every 6th row 14 more times = 80 sts.

• For chest 38 - 1 st at beg and end of next row. Repeat this 3 more times every 4th row. Then repeat this every 6th row 13 more times = 84 sts.

• For chest 40 - 1 st at beg and end of next row. Repeat this every 6th row 12 more times. Then do the same increase 3 more times every 8th row = 86 sts. Incorporate new sts into Wave Stitch Pattern. After all increases are done, work even until piece measures 211/4 (211/4, 221/2)" from CO. Loosely bind off all stitches.

FINISHING

Block pieces to measurements. Sew shoulder seams leaving central 81/2 (9, 91/2)" open for neck. Set in sleeves. Sew side and sleeve seams.

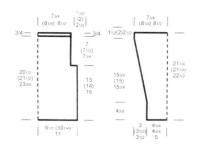

DELIZIOSA TEE
Continue from page 36

SHAPE SHOULDERS AND NECK

Next Row (RS): Bind off 5(5-6-6-7-9) sts, k until there are 10(12-14-16-18-18) sts on RH needle, join another hank of yarn and bind off center 30 sts, k to end. Working both sides at once, bind off 5(5-6-6-7-9) sts at beg of the next row, then 4(5-6-7-8-8) sts at beg of the next 4 rows. AT THE SAME TIME, dec 1 st at each neck edge EVERY row twice.

FRONT

Work same as back until armholes measure approximately 2(2-2 1/2-3-3 1/2-3 1/2)", end on WS. Mark the center 20 sts on needle.

Note: Work neck decs as SSK, k1 on left side of neck and as k1, k2 tog on right side of neck.

Shape Neck: Next Row (RS): Continuing to work armhole decs same as back if necessary, work to center 20 sts, join another hank of yarn and bind off center 20 sts, dropping markers, then work to end. Working both sides at once, continue to work armhole decs if necessary same as back. AT THE SAME TIME, dec 1 st at each neck edge as in note every RS row 7 times. When all decs have been completed, work even on 13(15-18-20-23-25) sts each side until armholes measure 7 1/2(7 1/2-8-8 1/2-9-9)", end on WS. Bind off 5(5-6-6-7-9) sts at each armhole edge once, then 4(5-6-7-8-8) sts twice for shoulders.

SLEEVES

With straight needles, cast on 60(60-66-70-76-80) sts. Work even in St st for 2", end on RS. Knit the next row on WS for Garter Ridge. Work even in St st until sleeve measures 3" from beg, end on WS.
Shape Cap: Bind off 5(5-7-9-10-11) sts at beg of the next 2 rows – 50(50-52-52-56-58) sts. Work 2 rows even.
Dec Row (RS): K2, k2 tog, k to last 4 sts, SSK, k2 – 48(48-50-50-54-56) sts. Rep this dec every 4th row 2(2-3-6-6-5) times more, then every RS row 14(14-12-6-6-8) times, end on WS – 16(16-20-26-30-30) sts. Bind off 3 sts at beg of the next 2 rows. Bind off remaining 10(10-14-20-24-24) sts.

FINISHING

Sew shoulder seams. Sew in sleeves. Sew side and sleeve seams.

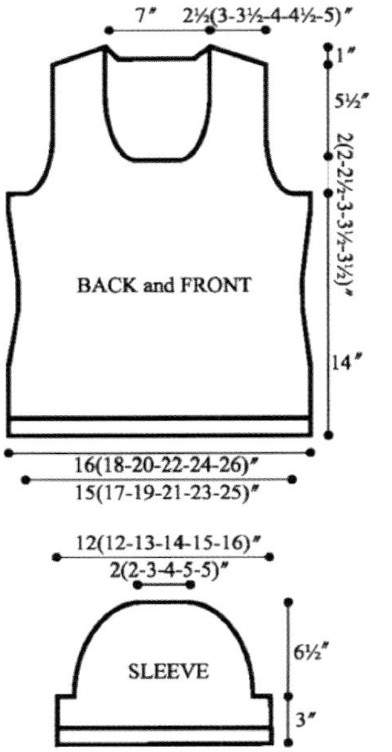
7"
2½(3-3½-4-4½-5)"
1"
5½"
2(2-2½-3-3½-3½)"
BACK and FRONT
14"
16(18-20-22-24-26)"
15(17-19-21-23-25)"
12(12-13-14-15-16)"
2(2-3-4-5-5)"
SLEEVE
6½"
3"

OPTIONAL PICOT CAST-ON EDGE

Using the cable cast-on technique, Cast-On **11 sts, bind off 4 sts as follows: Slip 1, slip 1, bind off 1. Then *slip 1, bind-off 1* 2x's more. Slip stitch on right needle back onto left needle** and repeat from ** - ** till you are at required cast-on total less 5 sts and have completed one last bobble, slip the one stitch left on right needle back to left needle and cast-on 5 more sts.

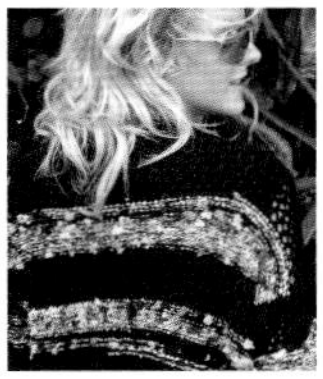

MINESTRONE & DOLCINO STRIPED JACKET

Continue from page 49

SLEEVES

Sew the shoulder seams closed. With #10 needle and Minestrone, Pick up 56(58,60,62)sts along the side edge from marker to marker. Work in Stripes as for the body changing yarns and patterns every 3" and at the same time decrease 1 stitch each end every 6th row 12(12,12,13)x. Continue until the sleeve is 15" from the pick up. Change to #9 needle and Dolcino in Rib St. for 2". Bind off in pattern. Repeat for other sleeve.

FINISHING

Sew the underarm and side seams closed. With #9 needle and Dolcino, Pick up 90(94,98,102)sts along the Left Front edge. Work in Rib St. for 1". Bind off. Place buttons evenly spaced along the Left Front and count stitches between buttons. With #9 needle and Dolcino, Pick up 90(94,98,102)sts along the Rt. Front edge. Work in Rib St. as counted from the left front, binding off stitches to match width of buttons at ½" from the pick up. Continue until the front band is 1". Bind off in pattern. With #9 needle and Dolcino, Pick up 92 (92,96,96)sts around the neck edge. Work in Rib St. for 2". Bind off in pattern.

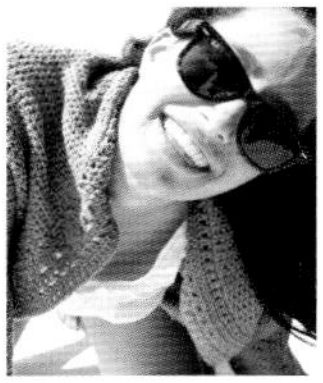

SHRUG ME!

Continue from page 50

BODY

Next Row (RS): Chain 17(18), join with a hdc in first hdc of sleeve, then continue to hdc in each hdc across sleeve, ch 20(21)
Following rows: Hdc in 3rd ch from hook and in next 17 (18) chs, hdc in each hdc across sleeve, hdc in next 18 (19) ch – 94(102)hdc. Ch 3, turn.
Repeat Row 6 of sleeve until piece measures 12"(14").
Double Crochet (dc) for the next 5".
Hdc for another 12"(14") – 29" (33") total.

RIGHT SLEEVE

Next Row (RS): Skip first 17(18) hdc, join with a slip stitch in next hdc, then hdc in next 57(63) hdc, leaving remaining 18(19) hdc unworked. Ch 2, turn.
Rows 1 and 2: Hdc in each st across.
Rows 3-4: Hdc2tog, hdc in each hdc to last 2hdc, hdc2tog -54(60). Ch 2, turn.

Patterns Continued

Rows 5-7: Hdc in each hdc across. Ch 2, turn.

Row 8: Hdc2tog, hdc in each hdc to last 2 hdc, hdc2tog – 52(58) hdc. Ch 2, turn.

Rows 9-11: Hdc in each hdc across. Ch 2, turn.

Rows 12-27: Repeat rows 6-9 four more times – 44(50) hdc. Ch 2, turn.

Row 28: Hdc across, decrease 6(8) hdc evenly spaced – 38(42). * Change to smaller hook, Ch 1, turn.

Row 29-32: Sc in each st across. Ch 1, turn

**When row 32 is completed, DO Not ch and turn: Fasten off

FINISHING
Sew side and sleeve seams.

BORDER
Foundation round: With RS facing, using larger crochet hook, join yarn with a slip stitch (sl st) in any side seam. Ch 1 (counts as 1 sc at side seam), work 128 (146) sc evenly spaced across to opposite side seam, sc in side seam, work another 128 (146) sc evenly spaced to beg. Side seam, join round with a sl st in beg ch1 0 258(294) sc.

Rnd 1: Ch 3 (always counts as 1 dc at side seam), ** dc in first st, skip next st, dc in next st, dc in skiped st, repeat from *62 (71) more times, dc in next st **, dc in next st at side seam, rep between **'s once more, join round with a sl st in 3rd ch of beg ch 3.

Rnd 2: Ch 2 (always counts as 1 hdc at side seam), hdc in each st around, join what a sl st in beg Ch 2.

Rnd 3: Ch 3, ** dc in first st, ch 1, * dc3tog, ch 2, rep from * 40 (46) times more, end dc3tog,
 ch 1, dc in next st**, dc in next st at side seam, rep between **'s once

more, join with a sl st in 3rd ch of beg ch 3.

Rnd 4: Ch 2, ** hdc in first st, hdc in ch 1 space, * hdc in next st, work 2 hdc in next ch 2 space, rep from * 40(46) times more, end hdc in next st, hdc in ch 1 space, hdc in next st **, hdc in next st at side seam, rep between **'s once more, join with a sl st in beg ch 1 space.

Rnd 5 and 6: Repeat Rnds 1 and 2.
Rnd 7: Sc in each stitch, fasten off.

WELLINGTON POLO PULLOVER
Continue from page 55

BEGIN SHOULDER SHAPING
Keeping in pattern BO 8 (10, 13, 15) sts loosely at begin of next 2 rows. Then BO 9 (11, 13, 15) sts loosely at beg of next 2 rows. Break yarn and put rem 40 (42, 42, 44) sts on a holder.

SLEEVES
With size 6 needle and (B), CO 46 (48, 50, 52) sts. Knit 1 row. Next row (RS): Change to (A) and starting with a knit row, work in stockinette using (A) for 7 rows, inc 1 st at each end of 3rd and foll 2 alt rows and ending after a RS row. 52 (54, 56, 58) sts. Work in pattern as stated for body, shaping sides of sleeve by inc 1 st at each end of 2nd and following 4 (5, 6, 7) alt rows, then on every 4th row until there are 84 (88, 92, 96) sts. Continue until work measures 17, 17 ¼, 17 ¾, 18) inches ending

after a WS row. Shape top of sleeves by keeping in pattern then BO 5 sts loosely at beg of next 2 rows. 74 (78, 82, 86) sts. Dec 1 st at each end of next and foll 3 alt rows. Then BO rem sts.

NECK SEAMING
Join right shoulder seam from armhole edge to sts on holder at neck edge. On RS facing and with size 6 needles and (B), knit across 40 (42, 42, 44) sts from front neck holder then knit across 40 (42, 42, 44) sts from back neck holder. BO on WS.

FINISHING
Join left shoulder and neck seam. Sew in sleeves. Seam sides. Steam lightly to block into shape.

TIMELESS HOURGLASS TANK
Continue from page 59

FRONT
Work as for back, including all hourglass, armhole and shoulder shaping. When piece measures 18 (18 ½, 18 ½, 19, 19) inches, shape for neck as follows: Place 11 sts from each shoulder onto 2 sep holders. Place center 46 (46, 50, 50, 54) sts on another holder. Work to center 14 (14, 18, 18, 22) sts, attach a second ball of yarn, BO center 14 (15, 16, 16, 16) st then complete remainder of row in pattern stitch. 27 stitches will remain on each side. Working both sides at once, Dec 1 st at each neck edge,

every row 16 (16, 16, 16, 16) times. Continue in pattern stitch until piece measures 23 (24, 24, 25, 25) inches from CO edge.

FINISHING

Seam shoulders and sides. Shape armholes as follows: with size 16 inch circular needle and RS facing, pick up 86 (92, 95, 102, 102) sts around perimeter of armhole opening. Adjust stitch count accordingly to work in 2 x 2 rib or desired edge for 1 ½ inches. BO in pattern loosely.

STANDARD NECK FINISHING

With size 16 inch circular needle and RS facing, pick up 134 (136, 138, 140, 140) sts around perimeter of neck opening. Inc or dec as necessary on the first row to balance pattern. Work in 2 x 2 rib for 1 inch or desired length. BO in pattern loosely. Gently block.

WORTH AVENUE WALKABOUT SWEATER

Continue from page 62

FINISHING Sew shoulders together.

SLEEVE TRIM

At marker, begin pick up 76 (79, 82) stitches around to other marker. Work 3X1 rib 8 rows. Bind off in patttern.
Sew sides and sleeves together.

YARN RESOURCES

ASLANTRENDS Invernal
50% Rabbit Angora 25% Merino Wool 25% Polyamide
Spun from the finest and most luxurious Angora rabbit from South America. Sublime!
 295 yards per skein

KOIGU Painter's Pallet Premium Merino (KPPPM)
100% Merino Wool
Each skein is a unique portrait of color. This yarn yields a gorgeous pair of socks but is also a fine choice for sweaters and shawls. Imported from Canada.
 175 yards per skein

LUCCI YARN Luca Tape
50% Viscose/35% Cotton/ 15% Polyester and Sequins
Truly a designer yarn. Multi-stranded with corresponding metallic & sequins.
 110 yards per skein

MALABRIGO Merino Worsted
100% Merino Wool from Uruguay
A sensuous and soft merino that absorbs the vibrant hand-painted colors created by the artisans of Malabrigo.
 210 yards per skein

MALABRIGO Silky Merino
50% Silk, 50% Baby Merino Wool from Uruguay
A luminous yarn amazingly dyed by the master colorists of the world-renowned Malabrigo Studios.
 150 yards per skein

MALABRIGO Rasta
100% Merino Wool, slightly felted from Uruguay. A soft, unplied, super bulky hand-dye available in over a dozen drenched colorways.
 90 yards per skein

MALABRIGO Rios
100% Superwash Merino Wool from Uruguay. The twist and washability of such a soft merino, coupled with the saturated colorways that only Malabrigo can create keep this yarn in high demand.
 210 yards per skein

PAGEWOOD FARM Paparazzi and Silk Ribbon
100% Silk Ribbon
Hand-dyed ribbon comes both unadorned or as Paparazzi, embellished with hand tied designer fabric, beads, sequins and faux pearls.
 Silk Ribbon and Paparazzi both 35 yards per skein

PRISM Angora
100% French Angora
Lovely, soft and saturated with the artistry of Prism's hand-dyes.
 90 yards per skein

PRISM Bubbles
100% Nylon.
Hand-dyed by the legendary Laura Bryant of Prism Arts, Bubbles is a playful novelty yarn that adds texture and interest to any quality project.
 68 yards per skein

PRISM Dover
75% Nylon, 25% Rayon
A tubular encapsulated by a railroad yarn, Dover is an unusually constructed yarn that takes the colors differently in both attributes.
150 yards per skein

continued page 72

Gourmet Food Photography:
    www.istockphoto.com
    www.shutterstock.com

YARN RESOURCES

PRISM Galaxy
95% Nylon, 5% Metallic Polyester
This fanciful wide ribbon with metallic accents creates a beautiful trim or fringe.
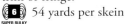 54 yards per skein

PRISM Kid Slique
66% Rayon, 26% Kid Mohair, 8% Nylon
Two strands of different fibers take the hand-dyes in a wonderfully lumi nous juxtaposition of color. A classic yet sophisticated Prism specialty yarn.
88 yards per skein

PRISM Velvet
100% Nylon
A ribbon with one soft plush, chenille edge, another unusual hand-dye Prism yarn.
88 yards per skein

ROBIN TURNER BACK TO BASICS' Prima Pima
100% Pima Cotton
An endearing classic, super soft with a non-pilling construction.
218 yards per skein

ROBIN TURNER BACK TO BASICS' MicroWash
100% Microfibre
Machine washable, dryer friendly. These attributes make MicroWash a popular staple for garments and décor for the entire family.
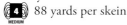 87 yards per ball

ROBIN TURNER GOURMET FIBERS' Bolivian Alpaca
100% De-haired Royal Alpaca
A Great Balls of Yarn favorite, super soft, lighter and warmer than cashmere.
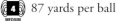 220 yards per skein

ROBIN TURNER GOURMET FIBERS' Deliziosa
100% Extrafine Superwash Lana Merino
Made in Italy exclusively for Great Balls of Yarn. The spin and color range of this irresistible merino make it a popular choice for a myriad of projects.
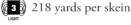 155 yards per ball

ROBIN TURNER GOURMET FIBERS' Heavenly Angora
80% Angora 10% Lana Wool 10% Nylon
Super soft angora in lovely colors with a touch of wool and nylon for stability.
165 yards per skein

ROBIN TURNER GOURMET FIBERS' Potpourri with Paillettes
Various compositions and blends of yarns with large paillettes stranded throughout a menagerie of color, texture and sparkle, Potpourri with Paillettes is made in small batches that cannot be replicated.
200 yards per skein

ROBIN TURNER GOURMET FIBERS' Silky Llama
Baby Llama 70% Mulberry Silk 30%
The highest quality silk spun with luxurious de-haired baby llama.
218 yards per skein

ROBIN TURNER GOURMET FIBERS' Soft Dreams
70% Extra Fine Kid Mohair 30% Silk
A lofty and luminous fine mohair that's gentle to the touch. A suitable choice for fine lace work yet also durable for sweater patterning.
230 yards ber ball

TRENDSETTER Cha Cha
47% Wool, 47% Acrylic, 6% Nylon
A versatile trim, knitting through top edge of each open box creates delicate ruffles, or one can simply knit with this wide ribbon, yielding a Berber effect.
65 yards per skein.

TRENDSETTER Dolcino
75% Acrylic/25% Nylon
Imported from Italy, this soft and pliable ribbon lends itself to virtually any couture project. A plethora of colors which correspond to the entire Trendsetter line.
100 yards per skein

TRENDSETTER Minestrone
75% Polyamide, 24% Acrylic, 1% Polyester Metalic
A glamorous, multi-textured yarn, Minestrone lends itself to many uses and is dyed to match other popular Trendsetter novelty yarns and self-ruffling varieties.
110 yards per skein

TRENDSETTER Tonalita
52% Wool, 48% Acrylic
Subtle color changes, terrific self-strip-ing, and superbly soft, a fabulous yarn that is dyed to match one of our very favorite yarns, Trendsetter Dune.
100 yards per ball